NEW JERSEY TRIVIA

COMPILED BY
ALBERT & SHIRLEY MENENDEZ

Rutledge Hill Press
Nashville, Tennessee

Published by Rutledge Hill Press, Inc.
211 Seventh Avenue North
Nashville, Tennessee 37219

Typography by D&T/Bailey Typography, Nashville, Tennessee

Library of Congress Cataloging-in-Publication Data

Menendez, Albert J.
  New Jersey trivia / compiled by Albert & Shirley Menendez.
      p.   cm.
  ISBN 1-55853-223-4 : $5.95
  1. New Jersey—Miscellanea.   I. Menendez, Shirley, 1937-
II. Title.
F134.5.M46   1993
974.9'0076—dc20   93-12564
                                                                    CIP

Printed in the United States of America
2 3 4 5 6—97 96 95 94 93

PREFACE

New Jersey is one of America's best kept secrets. A small state with remarkable diversity, it has a heritage and history well worth exploring. Its geography, leisure time activities, flora and fauna are among the subjects explored in this book.

In these pages you will discover, or rediscover, personalities such as Thomas Edison, Woodrow Wilson, Whitney Houston, Paul Robeson, Walter Schirra, Frank Sinatra, Meryl Streep, and others who have influenced their times.

It is our hope that both residents of and visitors to the Garden State will enjoy this journey through the history and literature of one of our nation's oldest and most interesting states.

Albert and Shirley Menendez

TABLE OF CONTENTS

GEOGRAPHY

Q. What fifty-two-room mansion in West Long Branch served as the Summer White House for Woodrow Wilson?

A. Shadow Lawn.

——————◆——————

Q. Near what town did Charles Lindbergh live when his son was kidnapped and murdered in 1932?

A. Hopewell.

——————◆——————

Q. Where did Aaron Burr mortally wound Alexander Hamilton in a duel on July 11, 1804?

A. Weehawken.

——————◆——————

Q. What is the narrow, sandy coastal island about thirty miles north of Atlantic City called?

A. Barnegat Light.

——————◆——————

Q. The Edison National Historic Site is situated in what town?

A. West Orange.

Q. New Jersey's highest altitude is at what place?

A. High Point in Sussex County.

———◆———

Q. What peninsula separates the Delaware Bay and the Atlantic Ocean?

A. Cape May.

———◆———

Q. How many steps lead to the top of Old Barney Lighthouse?

A. 217.

———◆———

Q. What town was informally nicknamed "the Irish Riviera"?

A. Spring Lake.

———◆———

Q. What county is largest in land area?

A. Burlington.

———◆———

Q. What old highway is the traditional route south from northern New Jersey to the shore?

A. Route 9.

———◆———

Q. Where are many black war veterans buried, including a sailor from the War of 1812?

A. Mount Pisgah Cemetery in Lawnside.

Q. Where is the Joyce Kilmer Oak?

A. On the Rutgers University campus in New Brunswick.

———◆———

Q. On what island is Atlantic City situated?

A. Absecon.

———◆———

Q. What West Orange neighborhood was planned and landscaped in the 1850s as America's first suburb?

A. Llewellyn Park.

———◆———

Q. The only access to Long Beach Island is over what bridge?

A. Manahawkin Bridge.

———◆———

Q. What fabulously wealthy woman owns a 6,000-acre estate in Somerville?

A. Doris Duke.

———◆———

Q. Grace Kelly had a summer home in what city?

A. Ocean City.

———◆———

Q. Situated within Jackson Township in Ocean County, what community is noted for its two Russian Orthodox churches?

A. Cassville.

Q. The Salvation Army's national headquarters is in what city?

A. Verona.

———◆———

Q. What islands were ceded to New York State in an 1833 treaty?

A. Liberty and Ellis.

———◆———

Q. What is the name of the pine forest that stretches nearly 2,000 square miles through central and southern New Jersey?

A. Pine Barrens.

———◆———

Q. What elegant village has estates belonging to the Dillons, the Forbeses, and Jane Engelhard?

A. Far Hills.

———◆———

Q. Which Hunterdon County town was once known as Skunk-town?

A. Sergeantsville.

———◆———

Q. Where in New Jersey can one take a Circle Line ferry to the Statue of Liberty?

A. Liberty State Park in Jersey City.

———◆———

Q. What town is on the New Jersey side of the Lincoln Tunnel?

A. Weehawken.

Q. The completion of which highway in the 1960s led to population growth in Sussex and Warren counties?

A. Interstate 80.

Q. What percentage of New Jersey is classified as "metropolitan" by the U.S. Census Bureau?

A. 100 percent, the most of any state.

Q. By what structure is Thomas Edison honored in Menlo Park?

A. A memorial tower is topped by a thirteen-foot replica of the first electric light bulb.

Q. Which New Jersey city has the largest land area, with sixty-nine square miles?

A. Vineland.

Q. For what multimillionaire is a park in Lakewood named?

A. John D. Rockefeller.

Q. According to the 1990 census, where does New Jersey rank in population?

A. Ninth.

Q. What resort town was founded in 1875 by Philadelphia department store magnate John Wanamaker and his friends?

A. Cape May Point.

Q. What city is the state capital?

A. Trenton.

———◆———

Q. How many public school districts does New Jersey have?

A. 585.

———◆———

Q. Which Morris County town is called "Rose City"?

A. Madison.

———◆———

Q. What town experienced a devastating fire in 1878?

A. Cape May.

———◆———

Q. Named for a television pioneer, what library is situated at 201 Washington Road in Princeton?

A. David Sarnoff Library.

———◆———

Q. The black Revolutionary War soldier Oliver Cromwell lived in what city?

A. Burlington.

———◆———

Q. In what Weehawken park is there a monument to and bronze bust of Alexander Hamilton?

A. Veterans Memorial Park.

Q. Until 1981, the governor's official residence was what mansion on Stockton Street at Library Plaza in Princeton?

A. Morven.

———◆———

Q. Where is Palmer Square?

A. Princeton.

———◆———

Q. What is New Jersey's nickname?

A. Garden State.

———◆———

Q. What town, just a footbridge across the Delaware River from New Hope, has many galleries and antique shops?

A. Lambertville.

———◆———

Q. What river flows through New Brunswick?

A. Raritan.

———◆———

Q. Which town in east central New Jersey became a resort center with such famous hotels as the Laurel House?

A. Lakewood.

———◆———

Q. Where does New Jersey rank in density of population?

A. First (with 1,042 people per square mile).

Q. What New Jersey highway is the most heavily traveled toll-road in the United States?

A. New Jersey Turnpike.

———◆———

Q. What town, settled by Moravians, is home to Sunrise Farms Christmas Shop?

A. Hope.

———◆———

Q. What small town is the county seat for Atlantic County?

A. Mays Landing.

———◆———

Q. The George Washington Bridge, linking Bergen County to Manhattan, opened in what year?

A. 1931.

———◆———

Q. Gertrude Ederle, the first woman to swim the English Channel, learned to swim in what town?

A. Highlands.

———◆———

Q. Which New Jersey county has the highest per capita income for the state?

A. Somerset ($32,469 in 1989 data).

———◆———

Q. Where does the Intracoastal Waterway begin?

A. Manasquan Inlet.

Q. What is New Jersey's largest state forest?

A. Wharton State Forest.

Q. What is the least populated county?

A. Salem.

Q. How many square miles of inland water does New Jersey have?

A. 319.

Q. Where is New Jersey's geographic center?

A. Mercer County, five miles southeast of Trenton.

Q. How many statute miles of Atlantic coastline does the state have?

A. 130.

Q. What coastal town is noted for its Victorian Christmas celebrations?

A. Cape May.

Q. What town is often called "America's most Hungarian city"?

A. New Brunswick.

Q. Stockton State College and the Atlantic City airport are in what town?

A. Pomona.

———◆———

Q. What city has the largest population in the state?

A. Newark.

———◆———

Q. What coastal city was established as a Methodist retreat center?

A. Ocean Grove.

———◆———

Q. A bronze statue honoring Thomas Paine is in what park?

A. Burnham in Morristown.

———◆———

Q. What ethnic group predominated Newark's old Central Ward?

A. Italian.

———◆———

Q. Where is the only U.S. Coast Guard station for training recruits?

A. Cape May.

———◆———

Q. What is New Jersey's largest lake?

A. Hopatcong.

Q. What sleepy town became bustling Jersey City?

A. Paulus Hook.

———◆———

Q. In what city are the corporate headquarters for Lenox China?

A. Lawrenceville.

———◆———

Q. The Outerbridge Crossing connects Staten Island with what New Jersey town?

A. Perth Amboy.

———◆———

Q. Which New Jersey town has the oldest Fourth of July parade in the state?

A. Florham Park.

———◆———

Q. The population of what Camden County town is 40 percent Jewish?

A. Cherry Hill.

———◆———

Q. What county has the largest population?

A. Bergen.

———◆———

Q. Where is Rutgers Law School?

A. Camden.

Q. Which bridge connecting New York and New Jersey has the nation's longest span for a vertical lift drawbridge?

A. Arthur Kill Bridge.

Q. What is New Jersey's northernmost county?

A. Sussex.

Q. The state's Atlantic beaches have been given what name?

A. The Jersey Shore.

Q. What deserted village near Stanhope has been restored and opened to the public?

A. Waterloo Village.

Q. Where is the headquarters of the National Religious Broadcasters?

A. Parsippany.

Q. What was Rutherford's original name?

A. Boiling Springs.

Q. Which Hudson County town was once notorious for its pig farms?

A. Secaucus.

Q. With a population of only 2,000, what is the state's smallest county seat?

A. May's Landing.

———◆———

Q. What is the name of the planned community in East Windsor Township?

A. Twin Rivers.

———◆———

Q. With only forty-six square miles, what is the smallest county in the state?

A. Hudson.

———◆———

Q. How many New Jersey cities had a 1990 population exceeding 100,000?

A. Four: Newark, Jersey City, Paterson, Elizabeth.

———◆———

Q. What immigrant group founded and shaped the culture of Egg Harbor City?

A. Germans.

———◆———

Q. When was the Palisades Interstate Park dedicated?

A. 1909.

———◆———

Q. New Jersey borders what states?

A. New York, Pennsylvania, and Delaware.

Q. Seven Presidents Park, named for the seven chief executives who summered there, is in what seacoast resort?

A. Long Branch.

Q. Where is Journal Square?

A. Jersey City.

Q. What two rivers almost meet twice?

A. Raritan and Passaic.

Q. What town was established as a kind of haven for writers and intellectuals?

A. Vineland.

Q. According to population, Newark has what rank among U.S. cities?

A. Fifty-third.

Q. Where was Sen. Frank Lautenberg born in 1924?

A. Paterson.

Q. When the state's first railway was completed in 1834, it connected what two towns?

A. Camden and Perth Amboy.

Q. What town is regarded as the seafood capital of the North Jersey Shore?

A. Highlands.

———◆———

Q. Where is the Bergen County Historical Society situated?

A. Steuben House in River Edge.

———◆———

Q. Which bridge connects Elizabeth and New York City?

A. Goethals Bridge.

———◆———

Q. What group operates a naval museum in Hackensack?

A. Submarine Memorial Association.

———◆———

Q. What is New Jersey's southernmost county?

A. Cape May.

———◆———

Q. Where is the second-largest waterfall in North America?

A. The Great Falls of the Passaic, a seventy-seven-foot high cascade.

———◆———

Q. A joint project of New Jersey and New York, the Holland Tunnel opened in what year?

A. 1927.

Q. What is the name of the museum of military life in Trenton?

A. Old Barracks Museum.

———◆———

Q. What two counties border Delaware Bay?

A. Salem and Cumberland.

———◆———

Q. What now-restored South Jersey site was once an industrial town noted for iron mining?

A. Batsto.

———◆———

Q. What state park is in Ocean County near New Gretna?

A. Bass River State Park.

———◆———

Q. The lighthouse at Barnegat Lighthouse State Park has what nickname?

A. Old Barney.

———◆———

Q. A favorite place for summer weddings is what mansion and gardens in Ringwood?

A. Skylands.

———◆———

Q. Where was Gen. Norman Schwartzkopf born on August 22, 1934?

A. Trenton.

Q. What are Loveladies, Harvey Cedars, and Ship Bottom?

A. Towns on Long Beach Island.

———◆———

Q. Which county has the highest percentage of persons age sixty-five years and over?

A. Ocean.

———◆———

Q. Ringwood State Park is in what mountain range?

A. Ramapo Mountains.

———◆———

Q. What cemetery in Passaic County is rumored to be haunted?

A. Ringwood Cemetery.

———◆———

Q. Where can a splendid Dutch windmill be seen in the rolling hills of Hunterdon County?

A. Volendam Windmill Museum.

———◆———

Q. Built in 1931, what 3,500-foot suspension bridge connects New Jersey and New York City?

A. George Washington Bridge.

———◆———

Q. Where does the Atlantic Ocean meet the Delaware Bay?

A. Cape May Point.

Q. Sen. Bill Bradley calls what town home?

A. Denville.

———◆———

Q. Which Princeton church was once pastored by Paul Robeson's father?

A. Witherspoon Presbyterian Church.

———◆———

Q. Where among the states does New Jersey rank in land area?

A. Forty-sixth.

———◆———

Q. Besides Newark, what New Jersey city is ranked among the top 100 in population in the United States?

A. Jersey City.

———◆———

Q. The Rabbinical College of America is in what city?

A. Morristown.

———◆———

Q. What name did Thomas Edison give to his twenty-three-room Victorian home?

A. Glenmont.

———◆———

Q. On their way to Europe in World War I, 40 percent of American soldiers passed through what New Jersey port?

A. Hoboken.

Q. Which summer resort town boasts two Christmas shops, Murdough's and the Paisley Christmas Shoppe?

A. Stone Harbor.

———◆———

Q. How many counties are in New Jersey?

A. Twenty-one.

———◆———

Q. What prevents New Jersey from being an island?

A. A forty-eight-mile boundary with New York.

———◆———

Q. The title "Blueberry Capital of the World" has been given to what city?

A. Hammonton.

———◆———

Q. When did the lighthouse at Cape May Point begin to guide vessels?

A. 1859.

———◆———

Q. The New Jersey Chamber of Commerce is in what city?

A. Newark.

———◆———

Q. What thirty-six-acre park is New Jersey's smallest state park?

A. Barnegat Light.

Q. The Graduate Record Examination Board has headquarters in what city?

A. Princeton.

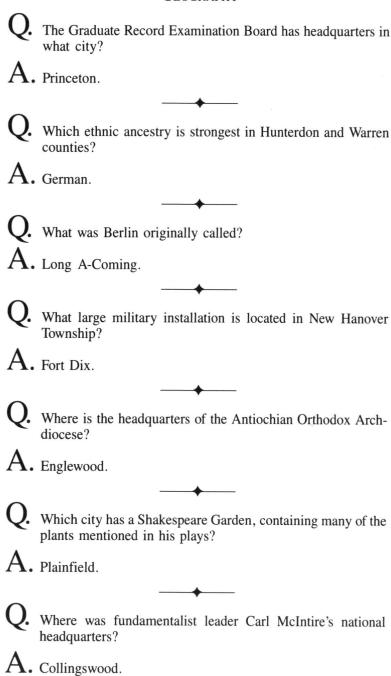

Q. Which ethnic ancestry is strongest in Hunterdon and Warren counties?

A. German.

Q. What was Berlin originally called?

A. Long A-Coming.

Q. What large military installation is located in New Hanover Township?

A. Fort Dix.

Q. Where is the headquarters of the Antiochian Orthodox Archdiocese?

A. Englewood.

Q. Which city has a Shakespeare Garden, containing many of the plants mentioned in his plays?

A. Plainfield.

Q. Where was fundamentalist leader Carl McIntire's national headquarters?

A. Collingswood.

Q. The *New Jersey Monthly* once called what town "the snootiest beach on the Jersey Shore"?

A. Bay Head.

———◆———

Q. Where is the headquarters of the New Jersey Bar Association?

A. New Brunswick.

———◆———

Q. The Cape May Ferry connects with what Delaware town?

A. Lewes.

———◆———

Q. What Ringwood man became geographer and Surveyor General to George Washington?

A. Robert Erskine.

———◆———

Q. The governor's "summer mansion" is in what state park?

A. Island Beach State Park.

———◆———

Q. Which county has the fewest people per square mile?

A. Salem.

———◆———

Q. Which state park is near Elmer?

A. Parvin State Park.

Q. People with Irish ancestry are the largest group in which county?

A. Cape May.

———◆———

Q. What organization is devoted to preserving local culture and traditions in the Pine Barrens?

A. Pinelands Cultural Society in Waretown.

———◆———

Q. The New Jersey Education Association has its headquarters in what city?

A. Trenton.

———◆———

Q. What New Jersey town is noted for the bold, contemporary architecture of its homes, most built since a 1962 storm?

A. Loveladies.

———◆———

Q. On Five Mile Beach, what towns are noted for their spectacular rides and amusement piers?

A. The Wildwoods.

———◆———

Q. What winery is the only one in the United States that makes blueberry champagne?

A. Renault Winery in Egg Harbor City.

———◆———

Q. Where was philanthropist Charles Stewart Mott born in 1875?

A. Newark.

Q. Where are the headquarters of the Blue Army of Our Lady of Fatima?

A. Washington, at the Shrine of the Immaculate Heart of Mary.

———◆———

Q. Which island was gradually destroyed by storms and eventually disappeared under the Atlantic Ocean in 1955?

A. Tucker's Island.

———◆———

Q. What restored nineteenth-century farm village is one-half mile north of the Cape May ferry landing?

A. Historic Cold Springs Village.

———◆———

Q. What southern New Jersey community was founded as a Utopian experiment in the nineteenth century?

A. Alliance.

———◆———

Q. People of English ancestry rank first in which New Jersey county?

A. Salem.

———◆———

Q. Where is the Naval Weapons Center?

A. Colts Neck.

———◆———

Q. The population of what county has the highest percentage of Italian ancestry?

A. Bergen.

Q. Among the states, where does New Jersey rank in per capita income?

A. Second.

———✦———

Q. James Fenimore Cooper's novel *The Water Witch* is set in what shore town?

A. Highlands.

———✦———

Q. What nationally known soup company has its headquarters in Camden?

A. Campbell's.

———✦———

Q. What Greek Revival mansion in Princeton is now the official residence of the governor?

A. Drumthwacket.

———✦———

Q. The writer Christopher Morley called what town "the last sea-coast of Bohemia"?

A. Hoboken.

———✦———

Q. What Monmouth County town was originally settled by Scots and called New Aberdeen?

A. Matawan.

———✦———

Q. Which county has the most people per square mile?

A. Hudson.

Q. What park is situated along the Black River in a gorge of exceptional beauty?

A. Hacklebarney State Park.

Q. America's oldest theological seminary is in what city?

A. New Brunswick.

Q. Confederate soldiers and German prisoners of war from World War II are buried in what cemetery near Salem?

A. Finn's Point National Cemetery.

Q. What is the only New Jersey town to have a neighborhood named after an American poet?

A. Matawan, where a section is named for Philip Freneau.

Q. On what river is New Brunswick situated?

A. Raritan River.

Q. What New Jersey canal, opened in 1834, once rivaled the Erie Canal as a commercial waterway?

A. Delaware and Raritan Canal.

Q. What state park in Highlands is built around a lighthouse?

A. Twin Lights Historic Site State Park.

Q. What resort town was founded by three brothers, all ministers?

A. Ocean City.

Q. Where is the Passaic County Historical Society housed?

A. Lambert Castle Museum in Paterson.

Q. What Hackensack cemetery contains the graves of nineteen soldiers of the Revolution, including Gen. Enoch Poor?

A. First Dutch Reformed Churchyard.

Q. What county has the largest Hispanic population?

A. Hudson.

Q. What turn-of-the century community devoted to cranberry and blueberry cultivation is now being restored as a historic area?

A. Whitesbog Village.

Q. Where did publisher Bernarr MacFadden die in 1958?

A. Jersey City.

Q. Before moving to Irving, Texas, the Boy Scouts of America had its headquarters in what New Jersey town?

A. New Brunswick.

Q. What New Jersey city lost more population during the 1980s than any other U.S. city except Gary, Indiana?

A. Newark.

———◆———

Q. President Bush made a campaign appearance at what Garfield church in 1992?

A. Three Saints Russian Orthodox Church.

———◆———

Q. What Somerset County village was the site of the first Lutheran Synod in America in 1735?

A. Pluckemin.

———◆———

Q. Maryland has the Preakness horse race, but which New Jersey County has a town named Preakness?

A. Passaic.

———◆———

Q. What was Rahway's original name?

A. Spanktown.

———◆———

Q. New Jersey's first Catholic community was organized in 1765 in which Passaic County village?

A. Macopin.

———◆———

Q. James Manning, the founder of Brown University, hailed from which New Jersey town?

A. Scotch Plains.

Q. Where was Benedict Arnold tried for treason in the winter of 1779?

A. Morristown at Dickerson's Tavern.

Q. Where did the zeppelin *Hindenburg* crash on May 6, 1937?

A. Lakehurst.

Q. The Delaware and Raritan Canal linked what two New Jersey cities?

A. Trenton and New Brunswick.

Q. Where did the trial of Bruno Hauptmann take place?

A. Flemington.

Q. Dating from the late eighteenth century, what community was incorporated in 1926 as one of the few all-black towns in America?

A. Lawnside, in Camden County.

Q. What two Hudson County towns have large Cuban–American communities?

A. West New York and Uniontown.

Q. What New Jersey county has the highest percentage of African Americans?

A. Essex.

Q. The name of what Hunterdon County town reflects its religious heritage?

A. Baptistown.

———◆———

Q. The U.S. Supreme Court required what resort town to sever its connections with the Methodist church, which controlled the local government?

A. Ocean Grove.

———◆———

Q. The first Indian reservation in the United States was established in 1758 in what Burlington County town?

A. Brotherton.

———◆———

Q. Near what appropriately named Ocean County town did a tragic 1854 shipwreck claim 354 lives?

A. Ship Bottom.

———◆———

Q. What ethnic group is predominant in South River?

A. Polish.

———◆———

Q. What county is home to twenty Fortune 500 companies?

A. Morris.

———◆———

Q. On which island are the resort towns of Avalon and Stone Harbor found?

A. Seven Mile Beach.

Q. What is the county seat of Sussex County?

A. Newton.

———◆———

Q. Which college is located on a wooded hilltop in the northeast corner of Wayne?

A. William Paterson State College.

———◆———

Q. What is Union County's smallest municipality in size and population.

A. Winfield.

———◆———

Q. Which Trenton building, completed in 1932, lies between the State House and the Delaware River?

A. War Memorial.

———◆———

Q. What town is situated at the mouth of the Navesink River?

A. Red Bank.

———◆———

Q. Which shore town is the site of the "Spy House," used by patriots during the Revolution?

A. Port Monmouth.

———◆———

Q. An estate in Peapack is owned by what former First Lady?

A. Jacqueline Kennedy Onassis.

ENTERTAINMENT

C H A P T E R   T W O

Q. What actor, who starred in *Fatal Attraction* and *Romancing the Stone,* was born in New Brunswick on September 25, 1944?

A. Michael Douglas.

◆

Q. Where does Eddie Murphy live?

A. Alpine.

◆

Q. What town on the New Jersey side of the George Washington Bridge was a movie production center from 1907 to 1916?

A. Fort Lee.

◆

Q. What zany comedian was born on March 16, 1926, in Newark?

A. Jerry Lewis.

◆

Q. What museum in Freehold celebrates the history of radio?

A. National Broadcasters Hall of Fame.

Q. At what Asbury Park club did Jon Bon Jovi and his band begin their career?

A. The Fast Lane.

———◆———

Q. What dancer made his debut in Keyport's Old Palace Theater in 1910?

A. Fred Astaire.

———◆———

Q. What famous theatrical family once owned a Victorian house at 2405 Hammet Avenue in Fort Lee?

A. The Barrymores.

———◆———

Q. Which actress and New Jersey resident is chairwoman of the New Jersey Film and Television Development Commission?

A. Celeste Holm.

———◆———

Q. Singer Sarah Vaughan is buried in what town?

A. Belleville.

———◆———

Q. Where was actor Ray Liotta born?

A. Union.

———◆———

Q. In 1941, what famous entertainer once worked as a fifty-dollar-a-week cocktail pianist at Pal's Cabin in West Orange?

A. Liberace.

Q. What is New Jersey's official state theater?

A. Paper Mill Playhouse in Millburn.

———◆———

Q. After Vanessa Williams resigned in 1984, which Mays Landing resident was named Miss America?

A. Suzette Charles.

———◆———

Q. Often called the "Empress of New Jersey," what singer owns a home in Glen Ridge?

A. Connie Francis.

———◆———

Q. Spring Lake served as a refuge for Patricia Neal in what sad 1968 film?

A. *The Subject Was Roses*.

———◆———

Q. A collection of aviation artifacts at the Teterboro Airport is named for what entertainer and flying enthusiast?

A. Arthur Godfrey.

———◆———

Q. Where did the world's first drive-in theater open on June 6, 1933?

A. Camden.

———◆———

Q. Magician David Copperfield was born in what town in 1957?

A. Metuchen.

Q. A Bertrand Island resident, who was Miss America in 1937?

A. Bette Cooper.

———◆———

Q. What was the Black Maria?

A. Thomas Edison's motion picture studio, based in New Jersey from 1893 to 1903.

———◆———

Q. What Spring Lake hotel was filmed in *Ragtime?*

A. The Essex–Sussex.

———◆———

Q. What old-time Hollywood comedian began his career as a juggler in Atlantic City?

A. W. C. Fields.

———◆———

Q. Opening in 1978, what was the first legal casino hotel in Atlantic City?

A. Merv Griffin's Resorts.

———◆———

Q. Songwriter Dorothy Fields was born in 1905 in what town?

A. Allenhurst.

———◆———

Q. Where is Elsie the Cow buried?

A. Plainsboro.

Q. What kind of music is played at the Yellow Rose in Manville and at the Silver Rose in Westville?

A. Country and western.

Q. What was the setting of the 1989 film *Penn and Teller Get Killed?*

A. Atlantic City.

Q. Lou Costello was born in what city?

A. Paterson.

Q. In which Woody Allen film were some scenes shot at Bertrand Island's Amusement Park in Mount Arlington?

A. *The Purple Rose of Cairo.*

Q. In 1980, the first installment of *Friday the 13th* was filmed in what town?

A. Blairstown.

Q. What 1985 film starring Rosanna Arquette and Madonna was shot at several New Jersey locations?

A. *Desperately Seeking Susan.*

Q. Who directed the 1980 film *Atlantic City?*

A. Louis Malle.

Q. What Nutley-born actor won an Emmy for "Baretta" in 1975?

A. Robert Blake.

———————◆———————

Q. What dancer for the American Ballet Company died in Hoboken on December 29, 1987?

A. Patrick Bissell.

———————◆———————

Q. What jazz pianist and songwriter died in Englewood in 1982?

A. Thelonius Monk.

———————◆———————

Q. Band leader and singer Jon Bon Jovi was born in which New Jersey town?

A. Sayreville.

———————◆———————

Q. Who wrote and directed *Return of the Secaucus Seven?*

A. John Sayles.

———————◆———————

Q. What Newark-born actor played James Evans on "Good Times" and Kunta Kinte in "Roots"?

A. John Amos.

———————◆———————

Q. Which star of TV's "Father Knows Best" was born in Campgaw in 1911?

A. Jane Wyatt.

Q. What choreographer, whose credits include *Funny Girl,* died at age thirty-nine in Saddle River?

A. Carol Haney.

———◆———

Q. What "swing-and-sway" band leader died in Ridgewood in 1987?

A. Sammy Kaye.

———◆———

Q. What large and impressive performing arts center is situated in Telegraph Hill Park in Holmdel?

A. Garden State Arts Center.

———◆———

Q. What fearsome figure of folklore is said to haunt the Pine Barrens?

A. The Jersey Devil.

———◆———

Q. Which Jersey Shore town has a remarkable carousel?

A. Seaside Heights.

———◆———

Q. Where was astrologer Carroll Righter born in 1900?

A. Salem.

———◆———

Q. Actor Sterling Hayden was born in which New Jersey town?

A. Montclair.

Q. The part of Rudy Huxtable on "The Cosby Show" was played by what Newark-born actress?

A. Keshia Knight Pulliam.

Q. Who was born at 415 Monroe Street in Hoboken?

A. Frank Sinatra.

Q. What elegant theater opened in Jersey City's Journal Square in 1929?

A. Loew's Jersey Theater.

Q. Which star of the TV show "M*A*S*H" owns a home at 18 Glenwood Avenue in Leonia?

A. Alan Alda.

Q. Summit is the hometown of what star of *Out of Africa* and *Sophie's Choice?*

A. Meryl Streep.

Q. The *Doonesbury* comic strip character Lacey Davenport is modeled on what pipe-smoking New Jersey congresswoman?

A. Millicent Fenwick.

Q. What band leader, who wrote the song "Toot, Toot, Tootsie, Goodbye," was born in Newark in 1900?

A. Ted Fiorito.

Q. Where was the Centaur Film Company based until it moved to Hollywood in 1911?

A. Bayonne.

Q. What 1903 silent film classic was filmed at the Edison Laboratory in West Orange?

A. *The Great Train Robbery.*

Q. Our Lady of Grace church in Hoboken was used for several scenes in what 1954 film?

A. *On the Waterfront.*

Q. What legendary circus impresario owned a house in Keyport?

A. P. T. Barnum.

Q. Asbury Park became a mecca for which kind of music during the 1960s?

A. Rock and roll.

Q. What composer lived at 84 Front Street in Red Bank around 1900?

A. John Philip Sousa.

Q. Western movie star Lee Van Cleef was born in what New Jersey town in 1925?

A. Somerville.

Q. In the 1920s many musicals bound for Broadway would try out in which Jersey town?

A. Atlantic City.

Q. Newark-born actress Vivian Blaine was noted for her role in stage and film versions of what musical?

A. *Guys and Dolls*.

Q. At what college were many scenes of the 1982 film *Annie* shot?

A. Monmouth College.

Q. Paterson school principal Joe Clark was the subject of what 1989 film?

A. *Lean on Me*.

Q. What native of Asbury Park organized the first U.S. fashion show in 1944?

A. Edna Woolman Chase.

Q. What comedic duo of the early screen were both New Jersey born?

A. Bud Abbott and Lou Costello.

Q. What Big Band vocalist and film star of the 1930s and 1940s was born in Atlantic City in 1918?

A. Helen Forrest.

Q. What diminutive character actor and director was born in Neptune and raised in Asbury Park?

A. Danny DeVito.

◆

Q. What 1986 film starring Melanie Griffith and Jeff Daniels was filmed throughout the state?

A. *Something Wild.*

◆

Q. Red Bank was the birthplace in 1904 of what Big Band leader?

A. Count Basie.

◆

Q. Where was Ozzie Nelson born in 1906?

A. Jersey City.

◆

Q. New Jerseyan Otto Messmer is best known for the creation of which cartoon character?

A. Felix the Cat.

◆

Q. Where was *The King of Marvin Gardens* filmed?

A. Atlantic City.

◆

Q. The role of Margaret ("Hot Lips") Houlihan on the television show "M*A*S*H" was played by what Passaic-born actress?

A. Loretta Swit.

Q. What charming monument to childhood was erected in 1930 in Hamburg?

A. The Gingerbread Castle.

———◆———

Q. What Fox TV series, about six single people sharing a New Jersey beach house, debuted on June 21, 1992?

A. "Down the Shore."

———◆———

Q. Ballerina Patricia McBride was born in what New Jersey town in 1942?

A. Teaneck.

———◆———

Q. Who wrote the song "Jeanie with the Light Brown Hair" while living at 601 Bloomfield Street in Hoboken?

A. Stephen Foster.

———◆———

Q. Nutley was the home of what sharpshooter from 1892 to 1913?

A. Annie Oakley.

———◆———

Q. From 1939 to 1944, Tenafly was home to what popular band leader whose plane mysteriously vanished during World War II?

A. Glenn Miller.

———◆———

Q. Famed cartoonist Thomas Nast owned a home called Villa Fontana in which north Jersey town?

A. Morristown.

Q. East Orange was the birthplace in 1941 of what Grammy-winning singer known for "That's What Friends Are For"?

A. Dionne Warwick.

Q. Wayne was home to what famed producer of epic films during his youth?

A. Cecil B. DeMille.

Q. What swing band leader lived on Old Army Road in Bernardsville from 1935 to 1941?

A. Tommy Dorsey.

Q. What singer, famous for "Garden Party" and "Poor Little Fool," was born in Teaneck in 1940?

A. Rick Nelson.

Q. Jersey City was the hometown of what singer noted for the song "These Boots Are Made for Walking"?

A. Nancy Sinatra.

Q. Where was actress Joan Bennett born in 1910?

A. Palisades.

Q. Which actor and singer who starred in *Oklahoma!* and *Carousel* was born in East Orange in 1921?

A. Gordon MacRae.

Q. Elizabeth was the 1892 birthplace of what actor whose best-known role was that of Scarlett O'Hara's father?

A. Thomas Mitchell.

◆

Q. What nineteenth-century violinist from the Pine Barrens is said to have played for the devil?

A. Fiddler Sammy Buck (Sam Giberson).

◆

Q. What actor, recipient of an Emmy in 1987 for "Moonlighting," grew up in Penns Grove?

A. Bruce Willis.

◆

Q. The music for "America the Beautiful" was composed by what Newark resident?

A. Samuel A. Ward.

◆

Q. What Atlantic City native wrote such songs as "I'm Always Chasing Rainbows" and "By the Beautiful Sea"?

A. Harry Carroll.

◆

Q. What Asbury Park club is called the "house that Bruce built"?

A. The Stone Pony.

◆

Q. What is the average daily win in Atlantic City's casinos?

A. Around $5 million.

Q. What actor, who starred in *Saturday Night Fever* and *Grease,* was born in Englewood in 1954?

A. John Travolta.

◆

Q. Comedian Flip Wilson was born in which large New Jersey city in 1933?

A. Jersey City.

◆

Q. What Oscar-winning actress, known for *On the Waterfront* and *North by Northwest,* was born in Newark in 1924?

A. Eva Marie Saint.

◆

Q. Freehold is the hometown for what singer known for the song "Born in the U.S.A."?

A. Bruce Springsteen.

◆

Q. What actor, winner of an Oscar for *One Flew Over the Cuckoo's Nest,* was born in Neptune in 1937?

A. Jack Nicholson.

◆

Q. What Jersey City-born actor played Theo Huxtable on "The Cosby Show"?

A. Malcolm-Jamal Warner.

◆

Q. What writer and TV show host once wrote a gossip column from Atlantic City?

A. Ed Sullivan.

Q. What unique tourist attraction is one mile south of Washington?

A. The Miniature Kingdom.

◆

Q. With space for 50 airplanes and 500 cars, a fly-in theater opened in 1948 in what coastal town?

A. Asbury Park.

◆

Q. A cocktail called the Jersey Devil contains what ingredients?

A. Cranberry juice, applejack, and rum.

◆

Q. Where can one hear folk music indigenous to the Pine Barrens?

A. Albert Hall in Waretown.

◆

Q. What renowned singer and dancer, born in Princeton, was valedictorian of his class at Rutgers?

A. Paul Robeson.

◆

Q. Which star of TV's "Crazy Like a Fox" was born in Newark in 1920?

A. Jack Warden.

◆

Q. What Jersey City-born singer performed with the Fifth Dimension from 1966 to 1973?

A. Marilyn McCoo.

Q. What actor, perhaps best remembered for his interpretation of Dracula, was born in Bayonne in 1940?

A. Frank Langella.

Q. In which posh town was *Prizzi's Honor* filmed?

A. Alpine.

Q. "Congress Hall March" was written in honor of a popular Cape May hotel by what famed bandmaster?

A. John Philip Sousa.

Q. Opera star Dorothy Kirsten was born in what New Jersey town in 1919?

A. Montclair.

Q. Brian Keith, who played Uncle Bill on TV's "Family Affair," was born in which north Jersey town in 1921?

A. Bayonne.

Q. What Camden-born actor was known for his portrayal of the Cisco Kid?

A. Duncan Renaldo.

Q. Born in Newark in 1937, what singer is noted for the song "My Eyes Adored You"?

A. Frankie Valli.

Q. Passaic was the birthplace of what actress who starred in *The Diary of Anne Frank* in 1959?

A. Millie Perkins.

Q. In what shore town was actor Preston Foster born in 1901?

A. Ocean City.

Q. What actress, born in Orange in 1922, played in the early TV series "My Favorite Husband"?

A. Joan Caulfield.

Q. Where did composer Roger Sessions die in 1985?

A. Princeton.

Q. Director Brian De Palma, whose credits include the movies *Carrie* and *Bonfire of the Vanities,* was born in what city in 1940?

A. Newark.

Q. Which Jersey City-born actress won a Tony in 1962 for *Subways Are for Sleeping?*

A. Phyllis Newman.

Q. Where was Martin Scorsese's *The Color of Money* filmed?

A. Atlantic City.

Q. What dancer, born in Jersey City in 1906, co-hosted with her dancer husband a popular television show in the 1950s?

A. Kathryn Murray.

Q. Where was Joe Piscopo born in 1951?

A. Passaic.

Q. What actor, born in Orange, was nominated for an Oscar for *All That Jazz* in 1979?

A. Roy Scheider.

Q. In what city was actor Jason Alexander born in 1959?

A. Newark.

Q. The 1992 movie epic *The Last of the Mohicans* was based on the novel by what Burlington-born nineteenth-century author?

A. James Fenimore Cooper.

Q. What singer and songwriter, born in Newark in 1942, won a Grammy for his album *Graceland?*

A. Paul Simon.

Q. Which star of the early TV show "Chance of a Lifetime" was born in Jersey City in 1917?

A. Dennis James.

Q. Where did English actress Wendy Barrie die in 1978?

A. Englewood.

———◆———

Q. What Morristown-born actress received an Oscar in 1983 for *The Year of Living Dangerously?*

A. Linda Hunt.

———◆———

Q. Named top female vocalist in 1986, what singer is a New Jersey native?

A. Whitney Houston.

———◆———

Q. What Newark-born singer sang the title song for the 1960 film *Where the Boys Are?*

A. Connie Francis.

———◆———

Q. Where was John Forsythe, star of "Bachelor Father" and "Dynasty," born in 1918?

A. Penns Grove.

———◆———

Q. In what small town was Mel Ferrer born in 1917?

A. Elberon.

———◆———

Q. What entrepreneur spent $1.3 billion to build the Taj Mahal Casino Hotel in Atlantic City?

A. Donald Trump.

Q. New Jersey-born Danny DeVito played which character on TV's "Taxi"?

A. Louis De Palma.

Q. Born in Bayonne in 1942, who was the star of *Gidget?*

A. Sandra Dee.

Q. Long Branch was the birthplace on February 4, 1962, of what singer noted for his hit "Put Yourself in My Shoes"?

A. Clint Black.

Q. Actor-director Roscoe Lee Browne was born in which New Jersey town in 1925?

A. Woodbury.

Q. Born in Hackensack in 1956, who was the original singer of "You Light Up My Life"?

A. Debby Boone.

Q. Where was *Married to the Mob* filmed in 1988?

A. South Hackensack.

Q. Known for her rendition of "Never Can Say Goodbye," who is the Newark-born "Queen of Disco"?

A. Gloria Gaynor.

Q. The New Jersey Shakespeare Festival is held in what town?

A. Madison.

◆

Q. Where is *Stages,* "the national theatre magazine," published?

A. Norwood.

◆

Q. What singer, famous for "Lonely Teardrops," died in Mount Holly in 1984?

A. Jackie Wilson.

◆

Q. New Jersey-born performer Juanita Hall played which character in *South Pacific?*

A. Bloody Mary.

◆

Q. What actor, born in Long Branch in 1926, played Oscar Goldman on "The Six Million Dollar Man"?

A. Richard Anderson.

◆

Q. Where was "Bullwinkle" cartoonist Al Kilgore born?

A. Newark.

◆

Q. What was the name of Fred Waring's Newark-born arranger?

A. Harry Simeone.

Q. What Belleville-born singer was one of the original members of The Four Seasons?

A. Tommy De Vito.

———◆———

Q. Where was television newsman Richard Valeriani born in 1932?

A. Camden.

———◆———

Q. Betsy Blair, born in Cliffside Park in 1923, was nominated for an Oscar for what 1955 film?

A. *Marty.*

———◆———

Q. What singer, born in Deal in 1956, married Bruce Springsteen?

A. Patty Scialfa.

———◆———

Q. Trish Van Devere, star of *Day of the Dolphin,* was born in what town in 1945?

A. Englewood Cliffs.

———◆———

Q. Where did *Topper* star Constance Bennett die in 1965?

A. Fort Dix.

———◆———

Q. What drummer, who played for the group Kool and the Gang, was born in Jersey City in 1949?

A. George Brown.

Q. Where does novelist and screenwriter John Sayles live?

A. Hoboken.

Q. Which star of *Call Northside 777* was born in Jersey City in 1914?

A. Richard Conte.

Q. In what city was Ernie Kovacs born in 1919?

A. Trenton.

Q. Which star of the early TV show "The Merry Mailman" was born in Jersey City in 1910?

A. Ray Heatherton.

Q. While living in a hotel in Atlantic City, what dancer-singer-composer wrote his autobiography *Twenty Years on Broadway?*

A. George M. Cohan.

Q. Where is the McCarter Theatre?

A. Princeton.

Q. Producer and screenwriter Dore Schary was born in 1905 in what city?

A. Newark.

Q. Born in New Jersey in 1952, who was the trombone player for Kool and the Gang?

A. Cliff Adams.

Q. Opera singer Frederica Von Stade was born in which Somerset County town in 1945?

A. Somerville.

Q. Where is the *Lottery Players' Magazine* published?

A. Cherry Hill.

Q. What black singer, actor, and political activist was born in Princeton in 1898?

A. Paul Robeson.

Q. Known for his portrayal of prissy hotel managers, what actor was born in Newark in 1894?

A. Franklin Pangborn.

Q. What modern dance pioneer and educator was born in Newark in 1877?

A. Ruth Saint Denis.

Q. "Who's the Boss?" star Judith Light was born in Trenton in what year?

A. 1950.

Q. What singer, born in North Bergen in 1929, starred on "Your Hit Parade"?

A. Tommy Leonetti.

Q. What Newark-born actor portrayed Neal Washington on "Hill Street Blues"?

A. Taurean Blacque.

Q. Born in Bound Brook, what actress played Megan Kendal on "Hotel"?

A. Heidi Bohay.

Q. Which lakeside town was a popular place for burlesque performers prior to World War I?

A. Hopatcong.

Q. The first symphony using jazz was written by what Trenton-born composer?

A. George Antheil.

Q. What songwriter, noted for "Look for the Silver Lining," attended Barringer High School in Newark?

A. Jerome Kern.

Q. Which museum has a collection of Annie Oakley mementos?

A. Nutley Museum.

Q. What art-filled mansion can be visited in Paterson?

A. Lambert Castle.

———◆———

Q. Where was producer-director Jean Dalrymple born in 1910?

A. Morristown.

———◆———

Q. Where did vaudevillian Joe Smith die in 1981 at the age of ninety-seven?

A. Englewood.

———◆———

Q. What Jersey City-born actor portrayed the Fernwood Flasher on "Mary Hartman, Mary Hartman"?

A. Victor Killian.

———◆———

Q. Which drummer for Duke Ellington was born in Long Branch in 1903?

A. Sonny Greer.

———◆———

Q. What is the name of Tiny Tim's former wife who now manages a luggage store in New Jersey?

A. "Miss Vicky" Budinger.

———◆———

Q. What Passaic-born producer won an Oscar for *Amadeus* in 1984?

A. Saul Zaentz.

Q. Where was early film star Norma Talmadge born in 1897?

A. Jersey City.

Q. Born in Newark in 1897, who composed the song "Tiptoe Through the Tulips"?

A. Nick Lucas.

Q. Actress Bibi Osterwald was born in 1920 in what city?

A. New Brunswick.

Q. What actor, who won an Obie for *Fool for Love,* was born in Englewood in 1950?

A. Ed Harris.

Q. What actress, born in Morristown in 1890, played Mother Dexter on "Phyllis"?

A. Judith Lowry.

Q. Where was Emmy-winning TV producer Gloria Monty born in 1921?

A. Union Hill.

Q. In which town was *On the Waterfront* filmed?

A. Hoboken.

Q. Lyricist Dory Previn was born in what New Jersey town in 1925?

A. Rahway.

Q. Columnist Dorothy Kilgallen's husband, writer Richard Kollmar, was born in what Bergen County town in 1910?

A. Ridgewood.

Q. Westfield was the birthplace of what cartoonist who drew a weird family?

A. Charles Samuel Addams.

Q. What musician, nicknamed "the Paganini of the Trombone," died in West Long Branch in 1942?

A. Arthur Pryor.

Q. Astrologer-magician "Amazing" Joseph Dunninger died in what New Jersey town in 1975?

A. Cliffside Park.

Q. Screenwriter Frances Goodrich, winner of a Tony for *Anne Frank* in 1956, was born in what city in 1891?

A. Belleville.

Q. Where was actor Philip Bosco born in 1930?

A. Jersey City.

Q. The bored housewife in *Desperately Seeking Susan* lived in what New Jersey town?

A. Fort Lee.

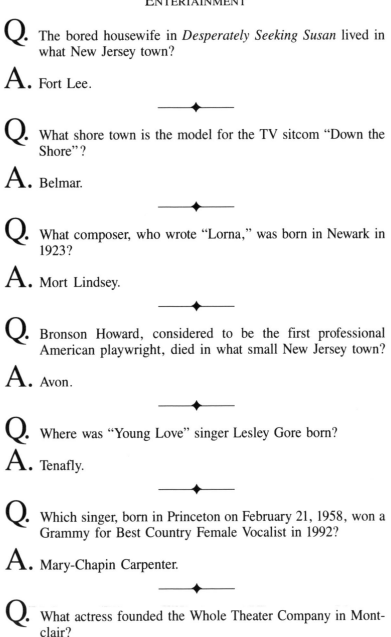

Q. What shore town is the model for the TV sitcom "Down the Shore"?

A. Belmar.

Q. What composer, who wrote "Lorna," was born in Newark in 1923?

A. Mort Lindsey.

Q. Bronson Howard, considered to be the first professional American playwright, died in what small New Jersey town?

A. Avon.

Q. Where was "Young Love" singer Lesley Gore born?

A. Tenafly.

Q. Which singer, born in Princeton on February 21, 1958, won a Grammy for Best Country Female Vocalist in 1992?

A. Mary-Chapin Carpenter.

Q. What actress founded the Whole Theater Company in Montclair?

A. Olympia Dukakis.

HISTORY

CHAPTER THREE

Q. What eminent New Jersey jurist served one of the longest terms on the U.S. Supreme Court, from 1956 to 1990?

A. William J. Brennan, Jr.

———◆———

Q. Ellesdale Manor Farm near South Branch was purchased by what financier and bon vivant in 1901?

A. Diamond Jim Brady.

———◆———

Q. What Revolutionary War pamphleteer lived in Bordentown from 1783 to 1787?

A. Thomas Paine.

———◆———

Q. What composer, who penned the hymn "Nearer My God to Thee," died in Orange in 1872?

A. Lowell Mason.

———◆———

Q. Who was the first Democrat to carry New Jersey for president since Lyndon Johnson in 1964?

A. Bill Clinton.

Q. What explorer of the West, for whom a Rocky mountain was named, was born in Lamberton in 1779?

A. Zebulon Pike.

———◆———

Q. Newark was the birthplace in 1756 of what brilliant but erratic vice president?

A. Aaron Burr.

———◆———

Q. The House Judiciary Committee was chaired by what New Jersey congressman during the impeachment hearings for Richard Nixon?

A. Peter Rodino.

———◆———

Q. Which feminist leader lived in Tenafly from 1868 to 1887?

A. Elizabeth Cady Stanton.

———◆———

Q. Orange was the birthplace in 1830 of what inventor who created a wide-brimmed hat?

A. John Stetson.

———◆———

Q. What antiwar activist and one-time New York congressman was born in Newark in 1929?

A. Allard Lowenstein.

———◆———

Q. The Democratic National Convention met in Atlantic City in what year?

A. 1964.

Q. What was New Jersey's first college for women, which opened in 1899?

A. College of St. Elizabeth at Convent Station.

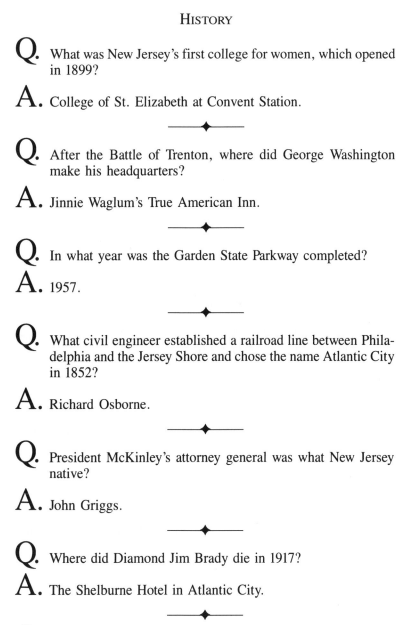

Q. After the Battle of Trenton, where did George Washington make his headquarters?

A. Jinnie Waglum's True American Inn.

Q. In what year was the Garden State Parkway completed?

A. 1957.

Q. What civil engineer established a railroad line between Philadelphia and the Jersey Shore and chose the name Atlantic City in 1852?

A. Richard Osborne.

Q. President McKinley's attorney general was what New Jersey native?

A. John Griggs.

Q. Where did Diamond Jim Brady die in 1917?

A. The Shelburne Hotel in Atlantic City.

Q. What New Jersey Democrat was elected governor three times, in 1925, 1931, and 1937?

A. A. Harry Moore.

Q. Who founded the Prudential Insurance Company in Newark in 1875?

A. John F. Dryden.

Q. Which president of Yale University was born in Morristown in 1906?

A. Whitney Griswold.

Q. Who was New Jersey's governor during the two world wars?

A. Walter Evans Edge.

Q. What Democratic senator, who served from 1959 to 1982, was convicted in the Abscam bribery scandal?

A. Harrison Williams.

Q. A California town is named for which Princeton-born naval officer?

A. Robert Stockton.

Q. The National Women's party was founded in 1913 by what long-time Moorestown resident?

A. Alice Paul.

Q. After fleeing persecution in England, what religious group settled Cohansey Corners (now Shiloh) in 1705?

A. Seventh Day Baptists.

Q. Who was the New Jersey woman whose parents won a landmark court decision in 1985 to remove her life support system?

A. Karen Ann Quinlan.

———◆———

Q. What controversial Franciscan priest and founder of Covenant House was born in Hamilton Township on February 25, 1927?

A. Father Bruce Ritter.

———◆———

Q. In 1992 who became the first Republican mayor of Jersey City in seventy-five years?

A. Bret Schundler.

———◆———

Q. The Declaration of Independence was signed by which New Jersey governor?

A. William Paterson.

———◆———

Q. What small museum in Haledon celebrates working-class immigrant life?

A. American Labor Museum.

———◆———

Q. How many people died in the 1967 riots in Newark?

A. Twenty-six.

———◆———

Q. What county has voted a Republican majority in every presidential election in this century except for 1964?

A. Ocean County.

Q. Which New York City mayor worked as a hatcheck boy in a Newark dance hall in his youth?

A. Ed Koch.

Q. In Elizabethtown in 1800, suffrage was extended to what group of people, whose right to vote was later rescinded in 1807?

A. Women.

Q. What percentage of New Jersey's residents are Jewish?

A. 4.3 percent.

Q. In which New Jersey community did Robert List murder his entire family one November day in 1971?

A. Westfield.

Q. A witch was tried in what New Jersey town in the 1730s?

A. Mount Holly.

Q. What Secaucus pig farmer ran for president twice as an Independent?

A. Henry Krajewski.

Q. What was Jimmy Carter's strongest New Jersey county in the 1976 presidential election?

A. Cumberland.

Q. What Democrat was sent to the U.S. Senate in 1863 even though he had been arrested for alleged disloyalty?

A. Col. James W. Wall.

◆

Q. In 1746, the first president of the College of New Jersey was what Presbyterian minister?

A. Jonathan Dickinson.

◆

Q. In what parish was New Jersey's first Catholic school opened in 1799?

A. St. John's in Trenton.

◆

Q. In what building did the Continental Congress meet from June until November 1783?

A. Nassau Hall at Princeton University.

◆

Q. The Pillar of Fire Church in Zarephath was founded by what colorful woman preacher?

A. Alma White.

◆

Q. When did New Jersey enter the Union?

A. December 18, 1787.

◆

Q. What Princeton-born commodore commanded the USS *Constitution* during the War of 1812?

A. William Bainbridge.

Q. Which Civil War general was governor of New Jersey from 1878 to 1881?

A. George B. McClellan.

---◆---

Q. What college was founded in Mahwah in the late 1960s?

A. Ramapo College of New Jersey.

---◆---

Q. In a letter opened after his death, what governor admitted to stealing $300,000 in state funds?

A. Harold G. Hoffman.

---◆---

Q. Federal Reserve Board chairman Paul Volcker was born in what town in 1927?

A. Cape May.

---◆---

Q. What speech writer for President Eisenhower was born in Newark and died in Princeton?

A. Emmet John Hughes.

---◆---

Q. Who was the legendary Pine Barren robber who preyed on settlers and was seized by vigilantes and hanged in 1781?

A. Joe Mulliner.

---◆---

Q. The secretary of the treasury under Presidents Kennedy and Johnson was what New Jersey resident?

A. C. Douglas Dillon.

Q. During what Revolutionary War battle did Molly Pitcher become famous for her courage and compassion?

A. Battle of Monmouth.

———◆———

Q. What New Jerseyan was president of the Continental Congress in 1783?

A. Elias Boudinot.

———◆———

Q. The tiny town of Coytesville was the 1892 birthplace of what U.S. admiral?

A. James Van Fleet.

———◆———

Q. What German-born British troops had their headquarters in New Jersey during the U.S. Revolutionary War?

A. Hessians.

———◆———

Q. What was the first New Jersey city to declare itself a nuclear-free zone in 1984?

A. Hoboken.

———◆———

Q. What lawyer successfully argued before the U.S. Supreme Court a case guaranteeing the right of a socialist to speak in public in Jersey City?

A. Arthur T. Vanderbilt.

———◆———

Q. The Seeing Eye organization for the visually impaired was established by what woman in Morristown in 1928?

A. Dorothy Harrison Eustis.

Q. What is the largest religious denomination in the state, with the allegiance of more than 40 percent of its residents?

A. Roman Catholic.

———◆———

Q. Who was Jersey City's long-time political boss and mayor from 1917 to 1947?

A. Frank Hague.

———◆———

Q. Where did President Wilson maintain his 1916 campaign headquarters?

A. West Long Branch.

———◆———

Q. How many members serve in the state's general assembly?

A. Eighty.

———◆———

Q. Who was the only New Jersey native to become president of the United States?

A. Grover Cleveland.

———◆———

Q. Where did U.S. president Lyndon Johnson and Soviet premier Aleksei Kosygin meet during their 1967 summit?

A. Glassboro State University.

———◆———

Q. The college that became Princeton University was founded in 1746 by what religious organization?

A. The Presbyterian Church.

Q. What U.S. steamer burned off the coast of Asbury Park on September 8, 1934?

A. *Morro Castle.*

Q. What secretary of labor under President Eisenhower was the GOP candidate for governor in 1961?

A. James P. Mitchell.

Q. What was the original name of Rutgers University?

A. Queen's College.

Q. In what numerical order did New Jersey enter the Union?

A. Third.

Q. What Quaker essayist, diarist, and strong opponent of slavery lived in Mount Holly?

A. John Woolman.

Q. What Princeton pioneer pollster founded the American Institute of Public Opinion?

A. George Gallup.

Q. How many members does New Jersey send to the U.S. House of Representatives?

A. Thirteen.

Q. What was New Jersey's first newspaper?

A. *New Jersey Gazette.*

------◆------

Q. In what numerical order did New Jersey ratify the Bill of Rights?

A. First.

------◆------

Q. What Republican was elected governor in 1969?

A. William T. Cahill.

------◆------

Q. The slogan "New Jersey and You, Perfect Together" was popularized by what governor?

A. Thomas Kean.

------◆------

Q. Whom did Robert Meyner defeat in the 1957 governor's race?

A. Malcolm Forbes.

------◆------

Q. Which nationally respected Republican senator was defeated for renomination in 1978?

A. Clifford Case.

------◆------

Q. What criminal was executed in Trenton on April 3, 1936, after a spectacular trial?

A. Bruno Hauptmann.

Q. New Jersey's worst train wreck killed eighty-four people on February 6, 1951, in what town?

A. Woodbridge.

———◆———

Q. Once considered the inventor of baseball, what Civil War general lived in Mendham?

A. Abner Doubleday.

———◆———

Q. What percentage of New Jersey's population is African American?

A. 13.4 percent.

———◆———

Q. What Jersey City college is the state's only Jesuit university?

A. St. Peter's College.

———◆———

Q. In what city was Adm. William ("Bull") Halsey born in 1882?

A. Elizabeth.

———◆———

Q. What part of Rutgers University was once the largest women's college in the United States?

A. Douglass College.

———◆———

Q. What is the state motto?

A. Liberty and Prosperity.

Q. For which governor is the Meadowlands sports arena named?

A. Brendan Byrne.

Q. The definitive study of the Underground Railroad was written in 1871 by what black businessman and Lawnside resident?

A. William Grant Still.

Q. Elizabeth was the home of what general in chief of the army and 1852 Democratic presidential candidate?

A. Winfield Scott.

Q. From 1881 to 1887, Trenton was the home of what mental health reformer?

A. Dorothea Dix.

Q. What Princeton man signed the Declaration of Independence?

A. Richard Stockton.

Q. A Victorian mansion in Summit was owned by what puritanical "vice suppressor"?

A. Anthony Comstock.

Q. How many congressional seats did New Jersey lose after the 1990 census?

A. One.

Q. Who was appointed New Jersey's last royal governor in 1763?

A. William Franklin, Benjamin Franklin's son.

---◆---

Q. Which political party won New Jersey's electoral votes for president for most of the nineteenth century?

A. Democratic.

---◆---

Q. What repository of New Jerseyana is situated in Newark?

A. New Jersey Historical Society.

---◆---

Q. Which candidate kicked off his 1980 presidential campaign at Liberty State Park in Jersey City on Labor Day?

A. Ronald Reagan.

---◆---

Q. In what building did the British surrender after the Battle of Princeton?

A. Nassau Hall.

---◆---

Q. Which former president died in Princeton in 1908?

A. Grover Cleveland.

---◆---

Q. Living in a slum in Hoboken, what woman miser amassed a fortune?

A. Hetty Green.

Q. For several years Princeton was home to what Soviet leader's daughter?

A. Svetlana Stalin.

Q. How many electoral votes does New Jersey cast for president?

A. Fifteen.

Q. Clara Barton, founder of the Red Cross, lived for a time in what city?

A. Bordentown.

Q. A substantial Portuguese population of 35,000 is found in what city?

A. Newark.

Q. Woodrow Wilson taught what subject at Princeton University?

A. Political science.

Q. What public servant was governor of New Jersey, superintendent of the U.S. Life Saving Service, and physician to President Lincoln?

A. William A. Newell.

Q. Franklin Park was the birthplace in 1904 of what U.S. senator?

A. Clifford Case.

Q. Caroline Fillmore, who married Millard Fillmore after his presidency, was born in which New Jersey town in 1813?

A. Morristown.

———◆———

Q. The second president of Princeton College was the father of what vice president?

A. Aaron Burr.

———◆———

Q. Roger Baldwin, founder of the American Civil Liberties Union, died in Ridgewood in what year?

A. 1981.

———◆———

Q. When did regular steamship connections between Cape May and Philadelphia begin?

A. 1819.

———◆———

Q. What missionary was active in Mount Holly from 1767 to 1775?

A. John Brainerd.

———◆———

Q. What Griggstown farmer was a spy for George Washington?

A. John Honeyman.

———◆———

Q. Who was the kidnapped Exxon executive found murdered in the Pine Barrens in June 1992?

A. Sidney J. Reso.

Q. Collingswood was the hometown of what national security adviser for President Reagan?

A. Richard Allen.

———◆———

Q. Anna Symmes Harrison, wife of one U.S. president and grandmother of another, was born in what town in 1775?

A. Morristown.

———◆———

Q. What congressman and Newark mayor was convicted of extortion in 1970?

A. Hugh Addonizio.

———◆———

Q. Albert E. Forsythe, the first black man to fly cross country, died in 1986 in what city?

A. Newark.

———◆———

Q. The president of Princeton University from 1902 to 1910 was what distinguished educator?

A. Woodrow Wilson.

———◆———

Q. Maywood in West Orange was the home of which Civil War general?

A. George B. McClellan.

———◆———

Q. A Georgian mansion at 435 Lydecker Street in Englewood was the home of what former U.S. ambassador to Mexico?

A. Dwight Morrow.

Q. When was the original colony of New Jersey divided into East and West Jersey?

A. 1676.

Q. What brewer built a Renaissance-style mansion in Newark in 1885?

A. John Ballantine.

Q. When was Rutgers University founded?

A. 1766.

Q. Morris and Sussex counties were the only ones in New Jersey to give a majority to which presidential candidate in 1992?

A. George Bush.

Q. During which decade did New Jersey's population increase by the greatest number?

A. 1950s.

Q. Where did Napoleon's brother Joseph Bonaparte live in New Jersey?

A. Bordentown.

Q. President Garfield died of wounds from an assassin in what New Jersey coastal village on September 19, 1881?

A. Elberon.

Q. Who narrowly beat James Florio in the 1981 governor's race?

A. Thomas Kean.

———◆———

Q. Who is the remarkable nurse and heroine of the Spanish–American War buried at Fairmount Cemetery in Newark?

A. Clara Maass.

———◆———

Q. New Jersey was the site of more than 100 battles and skirmishes in which war?

A. Revolutionary War.

———◆———

Q. For how many years each did Clifford Case and Harrison Williams represent New Jersey in the U.S. Senate?

A. Twenty-four.

———◆———

Q. What murder of a New Jersey clergyman and his paramour shocked the nation in 1922?

A. Hall–Mills Case.

———◆———

Q. Where does New Jersey rank among the states in expenditures per pupil in public schools?

A. First.

———◆———

Q. Which church in Swedesboro is called the Old Swedes Church?

A. Trinity Episcopal.

Q. What president, called the Father of the Constitution, studied at Princeton?

A. James Madison.

———◆———

Q. Which branch of the Algonquin Indian tribe lived in New Jersey?

A. Lenni Lenape.

———◆———

Q. What fur trader and millionaire built a summer mansion in Hoboken?

A. John Jacob Astor.

———◆———

Q. New Jersey was originally settled by what two European immigrant groups?

A. Swedes and Dutch.

———◆———

Q. What Democrat swept to easy gubernatorial victories in 1973 and 1977?

A. Brendan Byrne.

———◆———

Q. How many New Jerseyans died in World War II?

A. 10,372.

———◆———

Q. In 1890 and 1891, what president established his summer White House in the Cape May Congress Hotel?

A. Benjamin Harrison.

Q. What college was established in 1933 in West Long Branch?

A. Monmouth College.

———◆———

Q. In his *Old Guard* newspaper, what New Jersey publisher vilified President Lincoln?

A. C. Chauncey Burr.

———◆———

Q. Where does New Jersey rank in the percentage of its population that is foreign born?

A. Fifth, with 12.5 percent.

———◆———

Q. What colorful Republican congresswoman lost a tight U.S. Senate race to Frank Lautenberg in 1982?

A. Millicent Fenwick.

———◆———

Q. What New Jerseyan was secretary of the treasury under President Bush?

A. Nicholas F. Brady.

———◆———

Q. What relative of Franklin D. Roosevelt was the first Catholic bishop of Newark?

A. James Roosevelt Bayley.

———◆———

Q. With what denomination is the Old Scots Church, founded in 1692 in Freehold, associated?

A. Presbyterian.

Q. What one-time Camden laborer helped found the American Federation of Labor and fought for a national Labor Day holiday?

A. Peter McGuire.

———◆———

Q. From 1965 to 1967, what New Jerseyan served as President Lyndon Johnson's secretary of labor?

A. John T. Connor.

———◆———

Q. What New Jersey Federalist was the fourth Speaker of the U.S. House of Representatives from 1795 to 1799?

A. Jonathan Dayton.

———◆———

Q. President Franklin Roosevelt appointed which New Jersey governor as secretary of the navy in 1940?

A. Charles Edison.

———◆———

Q. A national Thanksgiving Day was proposed in an address on September 25, 1789, by what Elizabeth congressman?

A. Elias Boudinot.

———◆———

Q. In which New Jersey town did enraged colonists burn a supply of British tea one December night in 1774?

A. Greenwich.

———◆———

Q. When were the two Jerseys reunited as one colony?

A. 1702.

Q. What Salem County nurse was a beloved figure of compassion to the wounded troops at Gettysburg?

A. Cornelia Hancock.

———◆———

Q. America's first Episcopal bishop, Samuel Seabury, began his ministry at what church?

A. Christ Church, New Brunswick.

———◆———

Q. What college in Hackettstown opened its doors in 1867?

A. Centenary College.

———◆———

Q. Who was the only New Jersey resident to win the presidency?

A. Woodrow Wilson.

———◆———

Q. What was southwestern New Jersey called in the 1640s?

A. New Sweden.

———◆———

Q. Massachusetts congressman Barney Frank was born in 1940 in what city?

A. Bayonne.

———◆———

Q. How many New Jerseyans signed the Declaration of Independence?

A. Five.

Q. What New Jerseyan took the first U.S. Census of Religious Bodies in 1890?

A. Henry King Carroll.

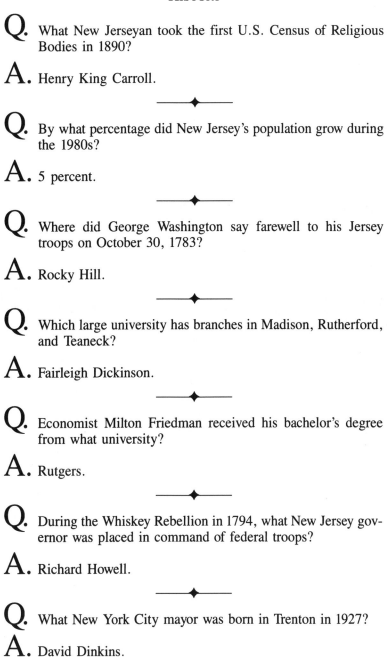

Q. By what percentage did New Jersey's population grow during the 1980s?

A. 5 percent.

Q. Where did George Washington say farewell to his Jersey troops on October 30, 1783?

A. Rocky Hill.

Q. Which large university has branches in Madison, Rutherford, and Teaneck?

A. Fairleigh Dickinson.

Q. Economist Milton Friedman received his bachelor's degree from what university?

A. Rutgers.

Q. During the Whiskey Rebellion in 1794, what New Jersey governor was placed in command of federal troops?

A. Richard Howell.

Q. What New York City mayor was born in Trenton in 1927?

A. David Dinkins.

Q. What private college is located in Lawrenceville?

A. Rider College.

———◆———

Q. What Jersey City political boss was deposed in 1969?

A. John V. Kenny.

———◆———

Q. What African American from Hackensack became executive assistant to President Eisenhower?

A. E. Frederick Morrow.

———◆———

Q. What controversial businessman served as President Reagan's first secretary of labor?

A. Raymond J. Donovan.

———◆———

Q. The town of Hope was founded in 1774 as a religious community by settlers of what denomination?

A. Moravians.

———◆———

Q. France's King Louis XVI once owned a garden in what Hudson County town?

A. North Bergen.

———◆———

Q. In what year was Bill Bradley elected to the U.S. Senate?

A. 1978.

Q. The 1946 and 1949 governor's races were won by what Republican?

A. Alfred Driscoll.

———◆———

Q. Elizabethport was the birthplace in 1891 of what U.S. Communist party leader?

A. Benjamin Gitlow.

———◆———

Q. The nickname "Brainy Borough" was given to what Middlesex County town because so many intellectuals lived there?

A. Metuchen.

———◆———

Q. How many members does the state senate have?

A. Forty.

———◆———

Q. In the late eighteenth century, what noted Methodist bishop significantly expanded church membership in the southern part of the state through the circuit-riding system?

A. Francis Asbury.

———◆———

Q. Where was Betsy Ross married?

A. Gloucester, in Huggs Tavern.

———◆———

Q. More New Jerseyans descend from what European ethnic group than any other?

A. Italian.

Q. In the 1864 presidential election, what New Jersey resident ran against Abraham Lincoln?

A. George B. McClellan.

———◆———

Q. What astute New Jersey political manager became Woodrow Wilson's trusted private secretary?

A. Joseph Tumulty.

———◆———

Q. Who commanded the First New Jersey Brigade in the Union army?

A. Gen. Philip Kearny.

———◆———

Q. The only clergyman to sign the Declaration of Independence was what New Jersey resident?

A. John Witherspoon, a Presbyterian minister.

———◆———

Q. The British burned what New Jersey town in 1782?

A. Toms River.

———◆———

Q. What Somerset County tavern keeper and horse thief became a spy for George Washington?

A. John Sutphen.

———◆———

Q. Where did bootlegger and racketeer Dutch Schultz die in 1935?

A. Newark.

Q. Until voters approved the new constitution in 1947, for how many years did New Jersey governors hold office?

A. Three.

———◆———

Q. After New Jersey separated from New York to become one of the original thirteen colonies, what two towns became joint capitals?

A. Perth Amboy and Burlington.

———◆———

Q. A Scottish immigrant, what general lost his life at the Battle of Trenton?

A. Hugh Mercer.

———◆———

Q. What former New Jersey governor committed suicide in 1931?

A. Edward I. Edwards.

———◆———

Q. George Washington selected what town for his army's winter quarters in 1776 and again in 1779–80?

A. Morristown.

———◆———

Q. Socialist leader Norman Thomas was barred from speaking at a public meeting in what municipality?

A. Jersey City.

———◆———

Q. What Princeton professor, clergyman, and author served as U.S. ambassador to the Netherlands from 1913 to 1916?

A. Henry Van Dyke.

Q. In 1912, President Taft appointed what New Jerseyan to the U.S. Supreme Court?

A. Mahlon Pitney.

◆

Q. What New Jersey conservative was secretary of the treasury in the Nixon and Ford administrations?

A. William E. Simon.

◆

Q. Who preached the frightful sermon "Sinners in the Hands of an Angry God" and was president of the College of New Jersey in 1757?

A. Jonathan Edwards.

◆

Q. Where are the headquarters for the U.S. Catholic Historical Society?

A. East Brunswick.

◆

Q. What U.S. senator from Florida was born in Atlantic City?

A. George Smathers.

◆

Q. A Reagan appointee, what conservative Supreme Court justice was born in Trenton in 1936?

A. Antonin Scalia.

◆

Q. Who is the legendary principal of Eastside High School in Paterson?

A. Joe Clark.

Q. Antiwar activist Mark Rudd was born in 1947 in what city?

A. Irvington.

———————◆———————

Q. What was the only New Jersey county to favor Al Smith for president in 1928?

A. Hudson.

———————◆———————

Q. What former actress and member of Congress, who ran against Richard Nixon for the U.S. Senate in 1950, was born in Boonton?

A. Helen Gahagan Douglas.

———————◆———————

Q. What is the annual salary for members of the state legislature?

A. $25,000.

———————◆———————

Q. James Birney, who ran for president twice on an antislavery ticket, died in what New Jersey town in 1857?

A. Perth Amboy.

———————◆———————

Q. In the 1980 presidential election, what county recorded the highest percentage of its voters for Independent candidate John Anderson?

A. Hunterdon.

———————◆———————

Q. In the presidential elections of 1860 and 1864, what candidate failed to carry New Jersey?

A. Abraham Lincoln.

Q. Pioneer pollster Archibald Crossley was born in what small New Jersey town in 1896?

A. Fieldsboro.

Q. Since World War II, what two Republican presidential candidates have carried every New Jersey county?

A. Eisenhower in 1956 and Nixon in 1972.

Q. Born in Newark in 1879, who founded the Big Brothers organization?

A. Irvin Westheimer.

Q. What Long Branch native died in office as vice president under William McKinley, to be succeeded by Theodore Roosevelt?

A. Garret Hobart.

Q. When was the New Jersey Historical Society founded?

A. 1845.

Q. What New Jerseyan served as President Eisenhower's secretary of labor for eight years?

A. James P. Mitchell.

Q. Where can one visit the U.S. Army Chaplain Museum?

A. Fort Monmouth.

Q. Who published New Jersey's first newspaper on December 5, 1777?

A. Isaac Collins.

———◆———

Q. In 1913, what psychological researcher published a startling report on "the Pineys," the poor people of the Pine Barrens?

A. Elizabeth Kite.

———◆———

Q. President Grant's two daughters attended what Episcopal school for girls in Burlington?

A. St. Mary's Hall.

———◆———

Q. What Mexican aviator, the Lindbergh of his country, died in a plane crash in the Pine Barrens on July 13, 1928?

A. Emilio Carranza.

———◆———

Q. Englewood was the birthplace on March 28, 1902, of what humanist philosopher?

A. Croliss Lamont.

———◆———

Q. Sailing vessels passing the Jersey Shore were preyed on by what celebrated thieves?

A. Barnegat Pirates.

———◆———

Q. In which month of 1962 was the Jersey Shore battered by a devastating storm?

A. March.

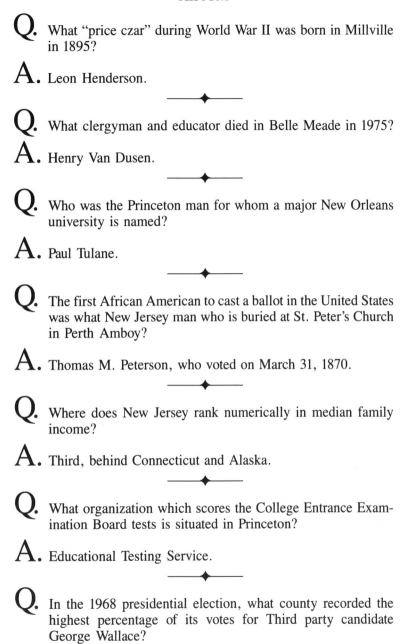

Q. What "price czar" during World War II was born in Millville in 1895?

A. Leon Henderson.

Q. What clergyman and educator died in Belle Meade in 1975?

A. Henry Van Dusen.

Q. Who was the Princeton man for whom a major New Orleans university is named?

A. Paul Tulane.

Q. The first African American to cast a ballot in the United States was what New Jersey man who is buried at St. Peter's Church in Perth Amboy?

A. Thomas M. Peterson, who voted on March 31, 1870.

Q. Where does New Jersey rank numerically in median family income?

A. Third, behind Connecticut and Alaska.

Q. What organization which scores the College Entrance Examination Board tests is situated in Princeton?

A. Educational Testing Service.

Q. In the 1968 presidential election, what county recorded the highest percentage of its votes for Third party candidate George Wallace?

A. Gloucester.

Q. In 1992, what Cuban American mayor of Union City became the state's first congressman of Hispanic descent?

A. Robert Menendez.

———◆———

Q. New Jersey received what nickname during the War of Independence?

A. Cockpit of the Revolution.

———◆———

Q. Earl Browder, leader of the U.S. Communist party from 1930 to 1945, died in what New Jersey town in 1975?

A. Princeton.

———◆———

Q. What English missionary is considered the father of the Episcopal church in New Jersey?

A. John Talbot.

———◆———

Q. In 1951, New Jersey nurse Clara Maass was honored with a postage stamp by which country?

A. Cuba.

———◆———

Q. Which two towns fought a hotly contested election in 1795 to become the county seat of Burlington County?

A. Mount Holly and Burlington (Mount Holly won).

———◆———

Q. What nineteenth-century women's rights activist lived in several New Jersey towns?

A. Lucy Stone.

Q. James Lawrence, a Burlington native who was captain of the USS *Chesapeake* in the War of 1812, uttered what immortal words?

A. "Don't give up the ship."

———◆———

Q. What Democrat was elected governor in 1961 and 1965?

A. Richard J. Hughes.

———◆———

Q. East Orange is the base for what Protestant federation?

A. New Jersey Council of Churches.

———◆———

Q. What U.S. diplomat, who developed the "good neighbor" policy in Latin America, died in Bernardsville in 1961?

A. Sumner Welles.

———◆———

Q. For what civil rights leader is Riverfront Park in Camden named?

A. Ulysses S. Wiggins.

———◆———

Q. Which railroad millionaire once operated a hotel in New Brunswick?

A. Cornelius Vanderbilt.

———◆———

Q. What personal secretary to Franklin Roosevelt was born in Bayonne in 1900?

A. Grace Tully.

Q. What New Jersey signer of the U.S. Constitution was appointed to the U.S. Supreme Court in 1793?

A. William Paterson.

✦

Q. Born in Chatham in 1843, what entrepreneur started America's first mail-order business?

A. Aaron Montgomery Ward.

✦

Q. The solidly Republican town of Saddle River is the home of what former Republican president?

A. Richard M. Nixon.

✦

Q. What was Princeton University's original name until 1896?

A. The College of New Jersey.

✦

Q. What was the only county in New Jersey to support Walter Mondale in the 1984 presidential election?

A. Essex.

✦

Q. How many times did presidential candidate Franklin Roosevelt carry New Jersey?

A. All four times.

✦

Q. While covering a silk workers' strike in 1913, what radical writer proclaimed, "There's a war in Paterson, New Jersey"?

A. John Reed.

Q. What New Jersey Democratic governor was considered a potential running mate for Adlai Stevenson in 1956?

A. Robert Meyner.

———◆———

Q. Who was Newark's first black mayor?

A. Kenneth Gibson.

———◆———

Q. Which religious group was prohibited from distributing Bibles in public schools by the New Jersey Supreme Court in 1951?

A. Gideon.

———◆———

Q. Which college is nicknamed Old Nassau?

A. Princeton.

———◆———

Q. When the New Jersey Turnpike was opened in 1952, who was governor of the state?

A. Alfred E. Driscoll.

———◆———

Q. What black physician in Mount Laurel attracted patients with his herbal medicine?

A. James Still.

———◆———

Q. To protect the interests of small states, the New Jersey Plan put forth at the 1787 Constitutional Convention advocated what legislative representation in Congress?

A. All states having equal representation (a compromise did this in the Senate but allowed the House to be based on population).

Q. "I am the boss" was the boast of what long-time Jersey City mayor?

A. Frank Hague.

---◆---

Q. Nicholas Murray Butler, winner of the 1931 Nobel Peace Prize, was born in what New Jersey town in 1862?

A. Elizabeth.

---◆---

Q. A bronze statue at Raritan commemorates what Guadalcanal hero from New Jersey?

A. John Basilone.

---◆---

Q. What Sussex County farm boy helped to lead Sherman's March to the Sea?

A. Hugh Hudson Kilpatrick.

---◆---

Q. With which denomination is the New Brunswick Seminary associated?

A. Reformed Church of America.

---◆---

Q. How many New Jerseyans fought for the Union during the Civil War?

A. 88,000.

---◆---

Q. Baptists fleeing religious persecution in Massachusetts founded what Monmouth County town?

A. Holmdel.

Q. What Elizabeth woman fought for prison reform and child welfare laws?

A. Emily Williamson.

———◆———

Q. Where did ammunition-laden railroad cars blow up on July 30, 1916?

A. Black Tom powder depot in Jersey City (German sabotage was suspected).

———◆———

Q. Which signer of the Declaration of Independence is buried at Old Friend's Burial Ground in Trenton?

A. George Clymer.

———◆———

Q. In what New Jersey town did Ross Perot campaign after the last presidential debate in 1992?

A. Flemington.

———◆———

Q. Which ecumenical religious organization, founded in 1962, is based in Princeton?

A. Consultation on Church Union.

———◆———

Q. What New Jersey town had attracted 950 Italian families by 1910, making it the most successful Italian American farming colony in the nation?

A. Vineland.

———◆———

Q. Which church in Union was the first building in New Jersey to be listed on the National Register of Historic Places?

A. Connecticut Farms Presbyterian Church.

ARTS & LITERATURE

CHAPTER FOUR

Q. What posh suburb of Newark is the setting for much of Philip Roth's novel *Goodbye, Columbus?*

A. Short Hills.

◆

Q. What author, whose works include *My Friend Flicka,* was born in Cape May Point in 1885?

A. Mary O'Hara.

◆

Q. What Anglo–American author wrote *The Cocktail Party* while living at 14 Alexander Street in Princeton?

A. T. S. Eliot.

◆

Q. In 1914, what was the first museum in New Jersey to open to the public?

A. Montclair Art Museum.

◆

Q. Born in Burlington, what early American author wrote *The Spy?*

A. James Fenimore Cooper.

Q. Now a National Historic Landmark, the house at 330 Mickle Street in Camden belonged to what poet?

A. Walt Whitman.

———◆———

Q. What chronicler of the Jazz Age arrived at Princeton as a freshman in 1913?

A. F. Scott Fitzgerald.

———◆———

Q. What columnist and author of satirical essays on urban life was born in Morristown in 1950?

A. Fran Lebowitz.

———◆———

Q. *East Wind over Weehawken* was painted by what artist?

A. Edward Hopper.

———◆———

Q. Gay Talese, author of *Honor Thy Father,* was born in 1932 in what city?

A. Ocean City.

———◆———

Q. Where is Stephen Crane, author of *The Red Badge of Courage,* buried?

A. Evergreen Cemetery in Hillside.

———◆———

Q. What New Jersey museum has a notable collection of Tibetan art?

A. Newark Museum.

Q. What is New Jersey's official state theater?

A. Paper Mill Playhouse in Millburn.

———◆———

Q. What town, conceived as a utopian community, is home to artist Ben Shahn?

A. Roosevelt.

———◆———

Q. Which Donald Westlake novel features John Dortmunder, a kidnapping, and a New Jersey setting?

A. *Jimmy the Kid.*

———◆———

Q. Who wrote a one-act play called *The Happy Journey to Trenton and Camden?*

A. Thornton Wilder.

———◆———

Q. The high-roller world of Atlantic City casino gambling is the setting for which Elmore Leonard novel?

A. *Glitz.*

———◆———

Q. "The Lady or the Tiger?" is the best-known short story by what nineteenth-century author who lived in Convent Station from 1881 to 1899?

A. Frank Stockton.

———◆———

Q. The eleven-volume series *The Story of Civilization* was written, in collaboration with his wife, Ariel, by what graduate of St. Peter's College?

A. Will Durant.

Q. What "word power" specialist died in Montclair in 1965?

A. Wilfred Funk.

———◆———

Q. What classic Wilfred Sheed satire on the writing life is set in New Jersey?

A. *The Hack.*

———◆———

Q. Who wrote his novel *The Adventures of Augie March* while he was a Creative Writing Fellow at Princeton?

A. Saul Bellow.

———◆———

Q. In what city did physician and poet William Carlos Williams live?

A. Rutherford.

———◆———

Q. Where was prolific author George Seldes born in 1890?

A. Alliance.

———◆———

Q. What author, who wrote the children's classic *Are You There God? It's Me, Margaret,* was born in Elizabeth in 1938?

A. Judy Blume.

———◆———

Q. In what building was author Stephen Crane born?

A. The parsonage of the Central Methodist Church, Newark.

Q. The 1934 Pulitzer Prize-winning poet Robert Hillyer was born in 1895 in what city?

A. East Orange.

———◆———

Q. What author, who wrote *The Other Wise Man,* is buried at Princeton Cemetery?

A. Henry Van Dyke.

———◆———

Q. *U.S. News & World Report* ranked what New Jersey college as "best buy" for inexpensive regional colleges in 1992?

A. Trenton State.

———◆———

Q. Who wrote the New Jersey-based suspense thriller *The Cradle Will Fall?*

A. Mary Higgins Clark.

———◆———

Q. Judith Viorst, poet and author of *People and Other Aggravations,* was born in Newark in what year?

A. 1931.

———◆———

Q. What irascible drama critic and member of the Algonquin Round Table, who inspired *The Man Who Came to Dinner,* was born in Holmdel in 1887?

A. Alexander Woollcott.

———◆———

Q. What is the title of the 1960 novel by Pietro Di Donato which concerns an Italian American family in West Hoboken during World War II?

A. *Three Circles of Light.*

Q. *The Day Lincoln Was Shot* was written by what Jersey City-born author?

A. Jim Bishop.

Q. In what year did author and reformer Upton Sinclair die in a New Jersey nursing home?

A. 1968.

Q. What nineteenth-century landscape painter spent his childhood in Newark?

A. George Inness.

Q. *Rescuing the Bible from Fundamentalism* was written by what outspoken Episcopal bishop of Newark?

A. John S. Spong.

Q. Which Ellery Queen mystery novel begins in a Trenton restaurant?

A. *Halfway House*.

Q. The address 120 Prospect Avenue, Princeton, was home to what poet who won the 1965 Pultizer Prize for *77 Dream Songs?*

A. John Berryman.

Q. The estate Sunnybank in Wayne was home to what author of *Lad, a Dog* and other stories about collies?

A. Albert Payson Terhune.

Q. Who wrote *The Jungle*, an exposé of the meat-packing industry, at a farm northwest of Princeton?

A. Upton Sinclair.

Q. In what city does the title character in Willa Cather's "Paul's Case" decide to commit suicide?

A. Newark.

Q. Who wrote *The Caballa* while teaching at Lawrenceville School?

A. Thornton Wilder.

Q. Glen Ridge was the birthplace in 1885 of what founder of *Business Week*?

A. Malcolm Muir.

Q. William Graham Summer, economist and author of *Folkways*, was born in Paterson and died in what city?

A. Englewood.

Q. At what address in Princeton would William Faulkner visit his editor Saxe Commins?

A. 85 Elm Road.

Q. In which New Jersey community does mystery writer Mary Higgins Clark own a home?

A. Saddle River.

Q. In the 1870s, what western writer of such places as Poker Flat and Roaring Camp came East and lived briefly at The Willows in Morristown?

A. Bret Harte.

———◆———

Q. Which publishing giant is based in New Providence?

A. R. R. Bowker.

———◆———

Q. What famous realistic artist of the sea painted Atlantic City's Absecon Lighthouse?

A. Winslow Homer.

———◆———

Q. What author of *Murder for Pleasure*, a classic history of mystery fiction, died in Highstown in 1991?

A. Howard Haycraft.

———◆———

Q. Which Princeton University library has three million volumes on its shelves?

A. Firestone Library.

———◆———

Q. Who wrote the first history of New Jersey, published in Burlington in 1765?

A. Samuel Smith.

———◆———

Q. Sculptor George Segal lives in what city?

A. South Brunswick.

Q. Who designed the first building at the Stevens Institute of Technology in Hoboken?

A. Richard Upjohn.

———◆———

Q. Margaret Sangster, author of *Good Manners for All Occasions*, died in Glen Ridge in what year?

A. 1912.

———◆———

Q. Which 1933 private-eye caper by John Katz is set in an affluent New Jersey town?

A. *Death by Station Wagon.*

———◆———

Q. Born in Alliance in 1893, who is the author of *The Seven Lively Arts?*

A. Gilbert Seldes.

———◆———

Q. An entertaining history of Atlantic City called *By the Beautiful Sea* was written by what author?

A. Charles E. Funnell.

———◆———

Q. What poet wrote that "China is nothing like New Jersey"?

A. Richard Wilbur.

———◆———

Q. What foremost American landscape designer laid out Cadwalader Park in Trenton in 1891?

A. Frederick Law Olmstead.

Q. Which Frederick Manfred novel is set in Passaic?

A. *The Brother*.

————◆————

Q. What New Jersey museum limits its collection to American art?

A. Montclair Art Museum.

————◆————

Q. Which Ocean County town is the home of the Garden State Philharmonic Symphony Orchestra?

A. Toms River. *

————◆————

Q. The publisher Prentice Hall, Inc., has its headquarters in what town?

A. Englewood Cliffs.

————◆————

Q. What 1965 mystery novel by Lillian O'Donnell is set in New Jersey?

A. *Babes in the Woods*.

————◆————

Q. What reporter for the *Newark Star Ledger* wrote *The Boys from New Jersey?*

A. Robert Rudolph.

————◆————

Q. What author, who wrote *Christmas Roses,* was born in Englewood in 1873?

A. Anne Douglas Sedgwick.

Q. Sylvia Beach, founder of a Paris bookshop and publisher of James Joyce's *Ulysses,* is buried in what New Jersey cemetery?

A. Princeton.

---◆---

Q. What poet, buried at Harleigh Cemetery in Camden, designed his own grave?

A. Walt Whitman.

---◆---

Q. The poet John Ciardi taught at what university from 1953 to 1961?

A. Rutgers.

---◆---

Q. Uncle Wiggily, the children's story character, was created by what Newark resident?

A. Howard R. Garis.

---◆---

Q. What poet and anthologist worked in his father's jewelry factory in Newark from 1902 to 1923?

A. Louis Untermeyer.

---◆---

Q. What long-time *Esquire* publisher died in Ridgewood in 1976?

A. Arnold Gingrich.

---◆---

Q. The faculty room at Princeton's Nassau Hall contains the painting of George Washington at the Battle of Princeton by what artist?

A. Charles Wilson Peale.

Q. The first chief of the music division at the Library of Congress was what native of Jersey City?

A. Oscar Sonneck.

＋

Q. What author of more than forty mysteries for young people, that used New Jersey settings, died in Seaside Park in 1950?

A. Augusta Seaman.

＋

Q. What Bordentown native is considered America's first woman sculptor?

A. Patience Wright.

＋

Q. Rex Beach, bestselling novelist of the 1920s and 1930s, died in what town?

A. Lake Hopatcong.

＋

Q. Red Bank was the birthplace of what eminent literary critic?

A. Edmund Wilson.

＋

Q. Which Picasso sculpture stands at the entrance to the Princeton University Art Museum?

A. *Head of a Woman.*

＋

Q. *Hans Brinker and the Silver Skates* was written by what Newark resident?

A. Mary Mapes Dodge.

Q. What 1969 Emma Lathen mystery novel is set in New Jersey?

A. *Murder to Go.*

Q. Frank Sheed, publisher and author of *Theology and Sanity,* died in what town in 1981?

A. Jersey City.

Q. Who was the first Resident Fellow in Creative Writing at Princeton University?

A. Allen Tate.

Q. What Princeton-born author wrote *The Pine Barrens* in 1968?

A. John McPhee.

Q. Where was poet and playwright Ntozake Shange born in 1948?

A. Trenton.

Q. The wedding of what renowned Scribners editor took place at the Church of the Holy Cross in Plainfield in 1910?

A. Maxwell Perkins.

Q. Philosopher and editor Paul Elmer More died in Princeton in what year?

A. 1937.

Q. What poet was almost drowned in the resort town of Point Pleasant in 1906?

A. Hilda Doolittle.

Q. Who wrote *Barnegat Pirates* in 1897?

A. Howard Van Sant.

Q. What long-time editor of *The Saturday Review* was born in Union Hill in 1912?

A. Norman Cousins.

Q. What explorer and painter of Indian life died in Jersey City in 1872?

A. George Catlin.

Q. Granville Hicks, proletarian author and former literary editor of the *New Masses,* died in which town in 1982?

A. Franklin Park.

Q. Poet Delmore Schwartz is buried in what New Jersey town?

A. Paramus.

Q. In which section of Newark did author Philip Roth and his character Alexander Portnoy grow up?

A. Weequahic.

Q. The noted southern author Peter Taylor was born in what New Jersey town in 1917?

A. Trenton.

Q. Dorothy Gilman, mystery writer and creator of the Mrs. Pollifax series, was born in what New Jersey town in 1923?

A. New Brunswick.

Q. Science fiction writer John W. Campbell was born in Newark and died in what small town?

A. Mountainside.

Q. Montclair was the last home of what publisher who established the Newbery and Caldecott medals?

A. Frederic Melcher.

Q. What world-renowned educator and philologist died in Glen Ridge in 1978?

A. Mario Pei.

Q. Born in Elizabeth in 1902, who was the author of *Valley Forge?*

A. Donald B. Chidsey.

Q. Where did author Louis Fischer die in 1970?

A. Hackensack.

Q. What Lutheran college in East Orange has a valuable collection of books on Scandinavian history and literature?

A. Upsala College.

———◆———

Q. Journalist Joseph Kraft was born in which New Jersey town in 1924?

A. South Orange.

———◆———

Q. What Frederick Buechner novel about an evangelical preacher in Princeton was published in 1974?

A. *Love Feast*.

———◆———

Q. The classic historical romance *Janice Meredith*, about New Jersey during the Revolution, was written by whom?

A. Paul Leicester Ford.

———◆———

Q. Which novel by Albert Idell concerns the railroad empires being constructed in New Jersey in the 1840s?

A. *Roger's Folly*.

———◆———

Q. Noted for her "advice to the lovelorn," what columnist died in Allendale in 1945?

A. Beatrice Fairfax.

———◆———

Q. Robert Molloy, author of the bestseller *Pride's Way*, lived in what New Jersey town?

A. Paramus.

Q. What 1931 novel by Jessie Fauset describes African American life in a New Jersey town?

A. *The Chinaberry Tree.*

◆

Q. What 1938 book by William Carlos Williams consists of short stories about a New Jersey physician who helps the poor?

A. *Life Along the Passaic River.*

◆

Q. Who wrote a humorous series of short stories called *Barnegat Ways* in 1931?

A. A. P. Richardson.

◆

Q. What German novelist lived at 65 Stockton Street in Princeton from 1938 to 1941?

A. Thomas Mann.

◆

Q. What journalist, who died in Princeton in 1983, was noted for his State of the Nation column?

A. Roscoe Drummond.

◆

Q. In an apparent suicide, what author of *The Native's Return* died at his home in Bloomsbury in 1951?

A. Louis Adamic.

◆

Q. What editor and folklorist wrote *The Roads of Home*, a folk history of the Garden State, in 1956?

A. Henry Charlton Beck.

Q. Fleming H. Revell, one of America's oldest religious publishers, once had its headquarters in what New Jersey town?

A. Old Tappan.

———◆———

Q. What New Jersey painter was called "the first great American landscape painter"?

A. George Inness.

———◆———

Q. Where is the famed Westminster Choir College?

A. Princeton.

———◆———

Q. What 1944 historical novel by Bruce Lancaster portrays the Battles of Princeton and Trenton?

A. *Trumpet to Arms.*

———◆———

Q. New England author Mary E. Wilkins Freeman died in what New Jersey town in 1930?

A. Metuchen.

———◆———

Q. In the early nineteenth century, what present-day industrial center attracted such literary figures as Washington Irving and William Cullen Bryant because of its pretty scenery?

A. Hoboken.

———◆———

Q. In his *Tales of a Wayside Inn,* Henry Wadsworth Longfellow told of the romance of what English girl who established a Quaker colony in New Jersey?

A. Elizabeth Haddon.

Q. What historian wrote *New Jersey and the Civil War?*

A. Earl Schenck Miers.

◆

Q. What editor and co-founder of *The Nation* lived in Orange?

A. Wendell Phillips Garrison.

◆

Q. *The Vanishing Hero* was written by what Irish writer while he was teaching at Princeton?

A. Sean O'Faolain.

◆

Q. Who wrote a 1940 novel called *Route 28,* about rich New Yorkers who flee to the Jersey countryside?

A. Ward Greene.

◆

Q. Which writer of hard-boiled mystery novels grew up in Elizabeth?

A. Mickey Spillane.

◆

Q. What Englewood-born woman was the daughter of a prominent U.S. diplomat, wife of a national hero, and a noted author in her own right?

A. Anne Morrow Lindbergh.

◆

Q. Whose murder in Weehawken on July 25, 1841, inspired Edgar Allan Poe's short story "The Mystery of Marie Roget"?

A. Mary Cecilia Rogers.

Q. Paulist Press, one of America's oldest Catholic publishers, is situated in what city?

A. Mahwah.

———◆———

Q. What writer established Helicon Hall in Englewood in 1906 as an experiment in communal living?

A. Upton Sinclair.

———◆———

Q. Where was author Waldo Frank born in 1899?

A. Long Branch.

———◆———

Q. What radical adventurer-journalist, who is buried in the Kremlin, attended Morristown School from 1904 to 1906?

A. John Reed.

———◆———

Q. *A. B. Bookman's Weekly,* the bible of the old-book trade, is published in what town?

A. Clifton.

———◆———

Q. What artist sketched the summertime activities at Long Branch for *Harper's Weekly?*

A. Winslow Homer.

———◆———

Q. What 1855 novel by Charles Peterson takes place in the Pine Barrens during the War of Independence?

A. *Kate Aylesford.*

Q. In 1925, Gertrude Atherton wrote what novel about Atlantic City?

A. *The Silver Cup.*

Q. What is generally considered to be the first novel with a New Jersey setting?

A. *Berkeley Hall,* published in London in 1796.

Q. What architect designed Johnson & Johnson's headquarters in New Brunswick?

A. I. M. Pei.

Q. What writer lived in a mansion called Linebrook in Princeton?

A. John O'Hara.

Q. What tree-loving poet has an avenue named for him in New Brunswick?

A. Joyce Kilmer.

Q. Who wrote *With Walt Whitman in Camden?*

A. Horace Traubel.

Q. Who wrote the intricate five-part poem "Paterson"?

A. William Carlos Williams.

Q. What English poet did some of his work in a study at 120 Broadmeade in Princeton?

A. Alfred Noyes.

Q. What author, who wrote *Our Town,* is buried at Mount Carmel Cemetery in Lyndhurst?

A. Thornton Wilder.

Q. Novelist Kay Boyle lived in what New Jersey town during her childhood?

A. Atlantic City.

Q. What short story writer, whose tales of the sea were popular, died in poverty in Atlantic City on March 24, 1915?

A. Morgan Robertson.

Q. What Scottish American suspense writer completed *While Still We Live* while living in Princeton?

A. Helen MacInnes.

Q. Where was Norman Mailer born in 1923?

A. Long Branch.

Q. What U.S. senator is the subject of John McPhee's 1965 book *A Sense of Where You Are?*

A. Bill Bradley.

Q. Who wrote *New Jersey's Historic Houses?*

A. Sibyl Groff.

———◆———

Q. Critic Leslie Fiedler was born in what city in 1917?

A. Newark.

———◆———

Q. Who wrote, "New Jersey has always been a useful no man's land between the arrogance of New York and the obstinacy of Pennsylvania"?

A. Struthers Burt.

———◆———

Q. Who established New Jersey's first printing press and publishing house in Woodbridge in 1751?

A. James Parker.

———◆———

Q. What playwright, born in Perth Amboy in 1766, is often called "the father of American drama"?

A. William Dunlap.

———◆———

Q. What early American poet died in 1832 near Freehold from exposure while returning from a tavern in a snowstorm at night?

A. Philip Freneau.

———◆———

Q. Ralph Ellison, author of *The Invisible Man,* taught at what New Jersey college?

A. Rutgers.

Q. What author ridiculed the headmaster at the Lawrenceville School, where he had taught, in his 1967 novel *The Eighth Day?*

A. Thornton Wilder.

Q. What novelist wrote about Hungarian and Bohemian immigrants in New Jersey?

A. Joseph Anthony.

Q. In 1973 who wrote a novel about a New Jersey nurseryman trying to protect his land from greedy developers?

A. Julian Moynahan.

Q. What Plainfield native, born in 1886, won the Pulitzer Prize for history in 1937 for *The Flowering of New England?*

A. Van Wyck Brooks.

Q. As a child, what playwright lived at 72 Boston Street in Newark?

A. LeRoi Jones (Imamu Amiri Baraka).

Q. What Paterson-born poet was a leading spokesman for the "beat" movement of the 1950s and the "hippie" movement of the 1960s?

A. Allen Ginsberg.

Q. What English novelist wrote *Take a Girl Like You* while he was a lecturer at Princeton?

A. Kingsley Amis.

Q. Who called New Jersey "a kind of no man's land between New York and Philadelphia"?

A. Edmund Wilson, in *The Nation,* June 14, 1922.

Q. Who completed his novel *Miss Lonelyhearts* at a hotel in Frenchtown?

A. Nathanael West.

Q. What New Jersey museum owns 150 etchings by Italian artist Piranesi?

A. Zimmerli Art Museum.

Q. What 1991 mystery novel by Sarah Shankman involves murder at the Miss America pageant?

A. *She Walks in Beauty.*

Q. David Taylor's 1954 novel *Lights Across the Delaware* depicts what New Jersey Revolutionary War battle?

A. Battle of Trenton.

Q. What death row inmate wrote *A Reasonable Doubt,* a powerful courtroom drama set in a New Jersey backwater town?

A. Edgar Smith.

Q. Who wrote *Princeton Stories* in 1902?

A. Jesse Lynch Williams.

Q. The title of what novel by Summit-born novelist Charles Jackson has entered the language to describe an alcoholic binge?

A. *The Lost Weekend.*

———◆———

Q. Where did bestselling novelist Joseph Hergesheimer live during the last decade of his life?

A. Stone Harbor.

———◆———

Q. Where was Howard Fast living when he wrote *The Passion of Sacco and Vanzetti?*

A. Teaneck.

———◆———

Q. Born in Union City in 1911, who wrote *Christ in Concrete?*

A. Pietro Di Donato.

———◆———

Q. Where was poet Elinor Wylie born?

A. Somerville.

———◆———

Q. What short story writer and witty member of the Algonquin Round Table was born in West End in 1893?

A. Dorothy Parker.

———◆———

Q. Where was Langston Hughes living when he wrote *Not Without Laughter?*

A. Westfield.

Q. The Red House at 145 Ewing Street in Princeton was home from 1956 to 1975 for what novelist?

A. Caroline Gordon.

———————◆———————

Q. Who wrote *Murder on the Palisades* in 1930?

A. Will Levinrew.

———————◆———————

Q. What Stephen Longstreet novel is based on the Hall–Mills murder case?

A. *The Crime*.

———————◆———————

Q. What Newark cathedral, situated at Clifton and Park avenues, is noted for its stained-glass windows?

A. Cathedral of the Sacred Heart.

———————◆———————

Q. Who wrote *Pictures from an Institution* while living in Princeton?

A. Randall Jarrell.

———————◆———————

Q. What novelist wrote about New Jersey pirates in his 1906 novel *The Tides of Barnegat?*

A. F. Hopkinson Smith.

———————◆———————

Q. The statuary in Military Park, Newark, includes a bust of John F. Kennedy by what major sculptor?

A. Jacques Lipchitz.

Q. What author of *My Pious Friends and Drunken Companions* was born in East Orange in 1888?

A. Frank Shay.

Q. Elizabeth was the birthplace in 1862 of what creator of the Rover Boys and the Tom Swift books?

A. Edward Stratemeyer.

Q. What long-time *New Yorker* writer and author of *Senator Joe McCarthy* was born in Jersey City in 1915?

A. Richard Rovere.

Q. What headmaster of a Catholic school in Hackensack greatly influenced F. Scott Fitzgerald?

A. Monsignor Sigourney Fay, to whom Fitzgerald dedicated *This Side of Paradise*.

Q. What writer wrote fondly of Princeton in his autobiography *And Gladly Teach?*

A. Bliss Perry.

Q. His experience on the assembly line at a Ford motor plant in Mahwah resulted in the 1957 novel *On the Line* by what writer?

A. Harvey Swados.

Q. Pirates on the Jersey coast were the subject for what Civil War admiral when he turned novelist?

A. David Dixon Porter.

Q. What 1969 novel by Phyllis Whitney takes place in New Jersey?

A. *The Winter People.*

Q. While he was living on a farm near Frenchtown, who wrote *Let Us Now Praise Famous Men?*

A. James Agee.

Q. What novelist used the Warford House Hotel in Frenchtown as a setting for his 1934 novel *A Cool Million?*

A. Nathanael West.

Q. Where did Frank and Lillian Gilbreth and their dozen children (immortalized in *Cheaper by the Dozen*) live?

A. Montclair.

Q. *Rousseau and Revolution* won a Pulitzer Prize in 1968 for what popular author of philosophy and history who lived for a time in Arlington and in Kearny?

A. Will Durant.

Q. What 1990 novel by Geoffrey Wolff portrays a modern Princeton student's life?

A. *Final Club.*

Q. Who wrote the "Lawrenceville Stories"?

A. Owen Johnson.

Q. In search of health, what Scottish-born author spent several months sailing in Manasquan in 1888?

A. Robert Louis Stevenson.

---◆---

Q. What essayist and trivia writer was born in Millville in 1865?

A. Logan Pearsall Smith.

---◆---

Q. Alexander Botts was the humorous creation of what Glen Ridge-born novelist?

A. William Hazlett Upson.

---◆---

Q. Which author of many books about the medieval world was born in Alpine in 1892?

A. Harold Lamb.

---◆---

Q. New Jersey's Lindbergh kidnapping case was the subject of what gripping 1991 novel by Max Allan Collins?

A. *Stolen Away.*

---◆---

Q. What nationally known group of Sherlock Holmes enthusiasts is based in Norwood?

A. Baker Street Irregulars.

---◆---

Q. Where was mystery writer Carolyn Wells born?

A. Rahway.

Q. Agnes Sligh Turnbull, author of many historical novels, lived in what city for sixty years?

A. Maplewood.

Q. Samm Sinclair Baker, co-author of *The Scarsdale Medical Diet,* was born in which New Jersey town in 1909?

A. Paterson.

Q. Of interest to Americans of Welsh ancestry, what magazine is published in Basking Ridge?

A. *Ninnau.*

Q. What Newark-born playwright and screenwriter wrote *Act One?*

A. Dore Schary.

Q. Where was novelist Josephine Lawrence born in 1897?

A. Newark.

Q. Avalon, at 59 Bayard Lane in Princeton, was what author's home?

A. Henry Van Dyke.

Q. In the 1840s, what Shrewsbury-born traveler was one of the first Americans to explore, then write about, Mayan ruins in the Yucatan?

A. John Lloyd Stephens.

Q. Where is the *New Jersey Monthly* published?

A. Morristown.

◆

Q. What popular writer of biographical fiction, such as *Lust for Life*, once directed the Little Theatre at the Jewish Community Center in Jersey City?

A. Irving Stone.

◆

Q. What playwright briefly attended Lawrenceville School until he was expelled?

A. Edward Albee.

◆

Q. A 100-acre farm near Frenchtown was owned by what famed editor of a small-town Kansas newspaper?

A. William Allen White.

◆

Q. Where is author Maxwell Bodenheim buried?

A. Cedar Park Beth-el Cemetery in Paramus.

◆

Q. What 1951 novel by Francis T. Field deals with New Jersey politics?

A. *McDonough*.

◆

Q. What writer served as pastor of the Dutch Reformed Church in Belleville?

A. DeWitt Talmage.

Q. Who wrote the novel *The Saint and the Hunchback* while serving on the Princeton faculty?

A. Donald A. Stauffer.

Q. What Bret Harte short story takes place in Morristown?

A. "Thankful Blossom."

Q. From which educational institution did Philip Van Doren Stern graduate in 1924?

A. Rutgers University.

Q. In what Union County town did journalist and editor Arthur Brisbane live?

A. Scotch Plains.

Q. What magazine, "celebrating the spirit of the Jersey Shore," is published at Bay Head?

A. *Coast*.

Q. What novelist owned a home in Hampton?

A. Glenway Westcott.

Q. Who wrote *Liberty Tavern*, a novel about New Jersey during the American Revolution?

A. Thomas Fleming.

Q. What English romantic poet has a national society dedicated to his memory with headquarters in Collingswood?

A. Lord Byron.

———◆———

Q. Where did Scribner's editor Maxwell Perkins, who was an important influence on novelist Thomas Wolfe, live as a young man?

A. Plainfield.

———◆———

Q. What nineteenth-century painter did some of his best work while residing at Eagleswood in Perth Amboy?

A. George Inness.

———◆———

Q. Where was Thornton Wilder's *Our Town* first performed on January 22, 1938?

A. Princeton's McCarter Theatre.

———◆———

Q. What fugitive poet-critic and his novelist wife lived in Princeton from 1939 to 1951?

A. Allen Tate and Caroline Gordon.

———◆———

Q. What poet and Dante translator lived in Metuchen?

A. John Ciardi.

———◆———

Q. In what New Jersey town did the poet-physician Thomas Dunn English reside?

A. Fort Lee.

SPORTS & LEISURE

C H A P T E R   F I V E

Q. What Syracuse star joined the New Jersey Nets in the 1990-91 season and averaged 10.3 rebounds per game?

A. Derrick Coleman.

———◆———

Q. What great old-time amusement park delighted visitors to Irvington from 1887 to 1965?

A. Olympic Park.

———◆———

Q. What Washington Redskins quarterback from 1971 to 1985 was born in New Brunswick in 1949?

A. Joe Theismann.

———◆———

Q. What was the name of the baseball field in Hoboken where the first game played with definite rules took place in 1846?

A. Elysian Fields.

———◆———

Q. What New Jersey Nets player scored the most points in the 1990–91 season?

A. Reggie Theus.

Q. What major league catcher was a *magna cum laude* graduate of Princeton and a Newark native?

A. Moe Berg.

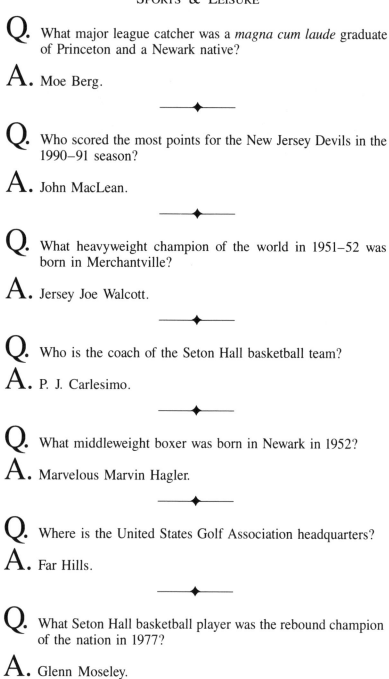

Q. Who scored the most points for the New Jersey Devils in the 1990–91 season?

A. John MacLean.

Q. What heavyweight champion of the world in 1951–52 was born in Merchantville?

A. Jersey Joe Walcott.

Q. Who is the coach of the Seton Hall basketball team?

A. P. J. Carlesimo.

Q. What middleweight boxer was born in Newark in 1952?

A. Marvelous Marvin Hagler.

Q. Where is the United States Golf Association headquarters?

A. Far Hills.

Q. What Seton Hall basketball player was the rebound champion of the nation in 1977?

A. Glenn Moseley.

Q. What popular board game uses Atlantic City locations?

A. Monopoly.

Q. What Princeton halfback won the Heisman Trophy in 1951?

A. Dick Kazmaier.

Q. What are the colors for the St. Peter's College basketball team?

A. Blue and white.

Q. In what town is the *Daily Racing Form* published?

A. Hightstown.

Q. What unusual sport is celebrated with a festival in Readington every July?

A. Ballooning.

Q. In which NBA league do the New Jersey Nets play?

A. Eastern Conference, Atlantic Division.

Q. The National Baseball Fan Association has its headquarters in what city?

A. Mount Laurel.

Q. What two New Jersey teams played the first college football game in 1869?

A. Rutgers and Princeton (Rutgers won, 6–4).

✦

Q. How many wineries are in the state?

A. Fifteen.

✦

Q. What Monmouth County town hosts the New Jersey Seafood Festival in June?

A. Belmar.

✦

Q. Where can one visit a museum dedicated to the history of soup?

A. Campbell Museum in Camden.

✦

Q. The Scarlet Knights is the nickname of what basketball team?

A. Rutgers.

✦

Q. The famous Boardwalk is found in what resort town?

A. Atlantic City.

✦

Q. What professional football coach lived in Englewood from 1939 to 1949?

A. Vince Lombardi.

Q. The Newton-based monthly, *Railroad Model Craftsman,* began publication in what year?

A. 1933.

Q. Where was Baltimore Oriole pitcher Bob Milacki born?

A. Trenton.

Q. What junior middleweight boxing champion died in Holmdel on June 3, 1988?

A. Davey Moore.

Q. What town, a mecca of malls, welcomed the Garden State Plaza in 1957?

A. Paramus.

Q. What legendary college football coach, at the University of Chicago for forty-one years, was born in West Orange in 1862?

A. Amos Alonzo Stagg.

Q. What is the nickname of the St. Peter's College basketball team?

A. The Peacocks.

Q. At what New Jersey sports facility do the New York Giants play their home games?

A. Giants Stadium in the Meadowlands Sports Complex.

Q. The list of top ten private courses compiled by *Golf Digest* included what golf course in Clementon?

A. Pine Valley Golf Club.

———◆———

Q. Where did Henry Ford and Louis Chevrolet stage an automobile race on the beach in 1905?

A. Cape May.

———◆———

Q. What Seton Hall basketball player scored 2,273 points during the 1962–64 seasons?

A. Nick Werkman.

———◆———

Q. During what month is Victorian Week celebrated at Cape May?

A. October.

———◆———

Q. What Trenton native pitched a no-hitter in his fourth appearance in the majors on May 5, 1962?

A. Bo Belinsky.

———◆———

Q. Dan Gutman, author of *Baseball Babylon,* lives in what city?

A. Haddonfield.

———◆———

Q. Where is the Cowboy Hall of Fame Restaurant and Saloon?

A. Bayville.

Q. What New Jersey-based basketball team had a forty-three-game winning streak during the years 1939–41?

A. Seton Hall.

Q. Where can one visit a fifty-acre flea market in which 700 vendors sell their wares?

A. Englishtown Auction.

Q. What is the nickname for Rider College's basketball team?

A. Broncos.

Q. What Newark-born National League baseball player was noted for his ability to steal bases?

A. Sliding Billy Hamilton.

Q. What popular magazine for golfers began publication in the late forties in Far Hills?

A. *Golf Journal*.

Q. Which New Jersey mall is one of the largest shopping centers in the United States?

A. Woodbridge Center in Woodbridge.

Q. What Jersey Shore town is synonymous with deep sea fishing?

A. Belmar.

Q. Built in 1898, what was Atlantic City's largest and most famous pier?

A. Steel Pier.

Q. What hockey coach, who led the Philadelphia Flyers to two Stanley Cup championships, died in Camden in 1991?

A. Fred Shero.

Q. What unusual fifty-member sports/religious organization has headquarters in Long Branch?

A. Racetrack Chaplaincy of America.

Q. *Craft and Needlework Age,* a monthly magazine, is based in small New Jersey town?

A. Englishtown.

Q. Where did the Dutch establish America's first brewery in 1642?

A. Hoboken.

Q. The great Brooklyn Dodger pitcher Don Newcombe was born in what New Jersey town in 1926?

A. Madison.

Q. Who wrote an 1889 guidebook called *The New Jersey Coast and Pines?*

A. Gustav Kobbe.

Q. Where was world-champion figure skater Elaine Zayak born in 1965?

A. Paramus.

Q. What zoo in Sussex County houses the world's largest Kodiak bear?

A. Space Farms.

Q. Where was the first baseball game played in the United States on June 19, 1846?

A. Hoboken.

Q. When was the first Miss America contest held in Atlantic City?

A. 1921.

Q. Even though his team posted the best record in its history in 1991–92, what New Jersey Devils coach was fired?

A. Tom McVie.

Q. Where was Baltimore Oriole outfielder Joe Orsulak born?

A. Glen Ridge.

Q. What college based in May's Landing has a Culinary Institute?

A. Atlantic Community College.

Q. What Atlantic City newspaperman originated the Miss America contest?

A. Herb Test.

◆

Q. The oldest rodeo on the East Coast is held at what location?

A. Cow Town in Sharptown.

◆

Q. What Hall of Fame baseball player, who had a lifetime .316 batting average, was born in Salem and died in Bridgeton?

A. Goose Goslin.

◆

Q. What popular candy has long been associated with Atlantic City?

A. Saltwater taffy.

◆

Q. Who is the general manager of the New Jersey Devils?

A. Lou Lamoriello.

◆

Q. In what year was the Princeton basketball team ranked third nationally?

A. 1965.

◆

Q. What zoo, the state's largest, has tried to exhibit many animals native to New Jersey?

A. Turtle Back Zoo in West Orange.

Q. What baseball player, born in Prospect Park in 1914, threw two consecutive no-hitters in 1938?

A. Johnny Vander Meer.

———◆———

Q. Basketball player and coach Al Attles was born in what city in 1936?

A. Newark.

———◆———

Q. What are Rider College's basketball team colors?

A. Purple and gold.

———◆———

Q. Who coached Seton Hall's basketball team, which went 28–2, in 1953?

A. Honey Russell.

———◆———

Q. What racing event is held each August at Meadowlands Racetrack?

A. Hambletonian Harness Racing Classic.

———◆———

Q. The Monmouth Hawks play in what basketball conference?

A. Northeast.

———◆———

Q. Where can one see the 6-iron used by astronaut Alan Shepard to hit a golf ball on the moon?

A. Golf House Museum and Library in Far Hills.

Q. Where is the *Tropical Fish Hobbyist* magazine published?

A. Neptune City.

◆

Q. Where was U.S. world champion figure skater Dick Button born in 1929?

A. Englewood.

◆

Q. When was gambling legalized in Atlantic City?

A. 1978.

◆

Q. The U.S. Baseball Federation is in which New Jersey town?

A. Trenton.

◆

Q. Tennis star Peter Fleming was born in what New Jersey town?

A. Summit.

◆

Q. In what year was Seton Hall ranked second in the final Associated Press basketball poll?

A. 1953.

◆

Q. Where does New York Mets infielder Willie Randolph live?

A. Franklin Lakes.

Q. The Meadowlands Sports Complex is in what city?

A. East Rutherford.

Q. What colors were adopted in 1965 as New Jersey's state colors?

A. Buff and blue.

Q. Pitcher Andy Messersmith was born in what New Jersey town?

A. Toms River.

Q. The Fairleigh Dickinson basketball team has what nickname?

A. The Knights.

Q. In what conference and division do the New Jersey Devils play?

A. Wales Conference, Patrick Division.

Q. What team beat Seton Hall, 80–79, in the 1989 NCAA college basketball championship?

A. Michigan.

Q. Who was named coach of the New Jersey Devils for the 1992–93 season?

A. Herb Brooks.

Q. For what team did Newark-born football player Drew Pearson play from 1973 to 1983?

A. Dallas Cowboys.

———◆———

Q. What 1978 Basketball Coach of the Year was born in Elizabeth?

A. Hubie Brown.

———◆———

Q. What Delaware River town celebrates the annual migration of shad fish with a festival each April?

A. Lambertville.

———◆———

Q. What New Jersey Nets player was named NBA Rookie of the Year for the 1990–91 season?

A. Derrick Coleman.

———◆———

Q. Camden native Mike Rozier won what coveted football award in 1983?

A. Heisman Trophy.

———◆———

Q. What is the nickname of Seton Hall's basketball team?

A. Pirates.

———◆———

Q. Brick is the location of what 400-member fan club?

A. Casino Chips and Gaming Tokens Collectors.

Q. What small Gloucester County town, settled by Finns in the late seventeenth century, is now a crafts and antique center?

A. Mullica Hill.

◆

Q. At Englishtown are the headquarters for what horseracing group?

A. Harness Horsemen International.

◆

Q. What Princeton basketball star was named the outstanding player in the 1965 Final Four?

A. Bill Bradley.

◆

Q. What kind of shopping is popular in Flemington?

A. Discount outlets.

◆

Q. When was the first Easter Parade held in Atlantic City?

A. 1876.

◆

Q. What amusement park in Jackson has seven roller coasters and the largest safari preserve in the United States?

A. Six Flags Great Adventure.

◆

Q. The Tile Fish Capital of the World is a title applied to what Jersey Shore town?

A. Barnegat Light.

Q. What is the venue for the National Hot Rod Association's annual July drag race?

A. Raceway Park in Englishtown/Old Bridge.

———◆———

Q. Pitcher Jim Bouton, a Newark native, wrote what bestseller in 1970?

A. *Ball Four.*

———◆———

Q. Harry Wright, who organized the first baseball team in Cincinnati in 1866, died in what New Jersey town?

A. Atlantic City.

———◆———

Q. What all-star forward for the Boston Celtics, 1957–1965, was born in Jersey City in 1934?

A. Tommy Heinsohn.

———◆———

Q. What pro football fan magazine is published in Red Bank?

A. *The Giants Newsweekly.*

———◆———

Q. What are the colors of Seton Hall's basketball team?

A. Blue and white.

———◆———

Q. What basketball coach and sportscaster was born in East Rutherford in 1940?

A. Dick Vitale.

Q. Where is the Garden State Park Racetrack?

A. Cherry Hill.

◆

Q. Where is Tofutti, the frozen tofu dessert company, situated?

A. Rahway.

◆

Q. Held in September with a purse of $350,000, what is the biggest race at Freehold Raceway?

A. James B. Dancer Memorial Race.

◆

Q. What was the name of an immensely popular amusement park in North Jersey?

A. Palisades Park.

◆

Q. What strange moveable conveyance was once a fad in Atlantic City?

A. Rolling Chair.

◆

Q. What village, just north of Interstate 80, near the Pennsylvania border, is devoted entirely to handcrafts?

A. Peters Valley.

◆

Q. What town holds a Cranberry Festival every October?

A. Chatsworth.

Q. The quarterly periodical *Bullpen* is published in Trenton by what organization?

A. Babe Ruth League.

◆

Q. Who replaced John Cunniff as manager of the New Jersey Devils on March 4, 1991?

A. Tom McVie.

◆

Q. What hockey player was killed in a car accident in Somerdale on November 12, 1985?

A. Pelle Lindbergh.

◆

Q. Where is the *National Speed Sport News* published?

A. Ridgewood.

◆

Q. Once the largest U.S. producer of champagne, what New Jersey winery opened in Egg Harbor City in 1864?

A. Renault Winery.

◆

Q. What Ocean County town is noted for cranberries, blueberries, and horse farms?

A. New Egypt.

◆

Q. What New Jersey racetrack is the oldest parimutuel harness track in the country?

A. Freehold.

Q. Photographs of Cape May often show what antiques shop?

A. The Pink House.

———◆———

Q. What racetrack in Oceanport features thoroughbred racing during the summer?

A. Monmouth Park.

———◆———

Q. What imaginative reconstruction of childhood characters is found in West Milford?

A. Fairy Tale Forest.

———◆———

Q. What Perth Amboy doctor invented a steerable balloon and tried to establish a balloon service between New York and Philadelphia?

A. Solomon Andrews.

———◆———

Q. Built in 1853, what Cape May hotel was considered the largest in the world?

A. The Mount Vernon.

———◆———

Q. What Hoboken man founded America's first yacht club and originated the America's Cup race?

A. John Cox Stevens.

———◆———

Q. Carteret was the birthplace in 1911 of which Hall of Fame baseball player?

A. Joe Medwick.

Q. What re-creation of an 1880 frontier town lies just east of Stanhope?

A. Wild West City.

———◆———

Q. Pro football Hall of Famer Jim Ringo was born in 1932 in what city?

A. Orange.

———◆———

Q. Where do the Howdy Doody Memorabilia Collectors have their headquarters?

A. Flemington.

———◆———

Q. What town celebrates a Tomato Festival each year?

A. Salem.

———◆———

Q. Each Memorial Day, what town hosts the oldest continuously run bicycle race in the country?

A. Somerville.

———◆———

Q. Who scored 41 goals for the New Jersey Devils during the 1991-92 season?

A. Claude Lemieux.

———◆———

Q. What is the venue for the only daytime harness racing in the United States?

A. Freehold Raceway.

Q. A National Historic Landmark, what whimsical six-story building constructed in 1881 of wood and tin can be toured at Margate?

A. Lucy the Elephant, complete with a canopied seat (howdah).

◆

Q. Where was golfing great Vic Ghezzi born in 1912?

A. Rumson.

◆

Q. The oldest snuff factory still operating in America is found in what Middlesex County hamlet?

A. Helmetta.

◆

Q. What Cape May hotel has long been known for its fine southern-style cooking?

A. Chalfonte.

◆

Q. Which coastal town has a Seashell Museum open Memorial Day to Labor Day?

A. Ocean City.

◆

Q. Where is the quarterly magazine *Bartender* published?

A. Liberty Corner.

◆

Q. George Hepbron, who wrote the first book about basketball in 1904, died in what New Jersey city in 1946?

A. Newark.

Q. For the past seven years, *New Jersey Monthly* has selected what New Brunswick restaurant as the Garden State's best?

A. The Frog and the Peach.

———◆———

Q. What New Jerseyan was point guard for the Duke Blue Devils in their 1991 and 1992 championship seasons?

A. Bobby Hurley.

———◆———

Q. What sport can be enjoyed at High Point, Stokes, and Swartswood state parks?

A. Cross-country skiing.

———◆———

Q. What famous Hoboken restaurant has been delighting food lovers since 1899?

A. Clam Broth House.

———◆———

Q. What replica of a Mississippi River paddleboat cruises the Manasquan River and Barnegat Bay?

A. *River Belle*.

———◆———

Q. Boat basins in Brielle and Point Pleasant sponsor what type of sporting event with thousands of dollars in cash prizes?

A. Shark fishing tournaments.

———◆———

Q. What is the name of the hair-raising roller coaster ride at Six Flags Great Adventure?

A. The Great American Scream Machine.

SCIENCE & NATURE

C H A P T E R   S I X

Q. What world-reknown scientist, who devised the formula E = mc^2, lived in Princeton from 1933 until his death in 1955?

A. Albert Einstein.

———◆———

Q. What New Jersey location has a large gull colony?

A. Nummy Island.

———◆———

Q. At what university was the drug streptomycin developed in 1943?

A. Rutgers.

———◆———

Q. What stunning wildflower blooms abundantly in the spring in Cheesequake State Park?

A. Pink lady's-slipper.

———◆———

Q. The Victrola, an early spring-cranked phonograph, was manufactured in what city?

A. Camden.

Q. What New Jersey winery made a "medicinal tonic" under a special government license during Prohibition?

A. Renault.

Q. What unusual facility in Forked River was founded by the Humane Society to house animals no one else wants?

A. Popcorn Park Zoo.

Q. The New Jersey Museum of Archaeology is at what Madison institution?

A. Drew University.

Q. Where is New Jersey's official botanical gardens?

A. Skylands, at Ringwood State Park.

Q. What New Jersey location is a popular place for snowy owls?

A. Sandy Hook.

Q. What 440-acre tract three miles from the main Princeton campus is a site for the university's advanced research in engineering sciences?

A. James Forrestal Campus.

Q. What Vineland dentist developed a nonfermentative method of preserving grape juice that permanently associated the product with his name?

A. T. B. Welch.

Q. What is the most common bird in the Pine Barrens?

A. The towhee.

———◆———

Q. Charles E. Hires, who devised the formula for root beer in 1876, was born in what small New Jersey community?

A. Roadstown.

———◆———

Q. Earle Dickson, who died in New Brunswick in 1961, was the inventor of what common first-aid product?

A. Band-Aid.

———◆———

Q. When did New Jersey become the first state to establish an endangered species project?

A. 1973.

———◆———

Q. At what New Jersey site was the first U.S. airship, the *Shenandoah,* based?

A. Lakehurst Naval Air Station.

———◆———

Q. What town is the home of the largest American holly farm in the United States?

A. Millville.

———◆———

Q. Where does the U.S. Army maintain an armament research and development center?

A. Picatinny Arsenal and Museum.

Q. What museum in Franklin celebrates three centuries of zinc mining?

A. Franklin Mineral Museum and Mine Replica.

Q. What part of New Jersey is said to have yielded a greater variety of minerals than any other on Earth?

A. Franklin–Ogdensburg area of eastern Sussex County.

Q. What Montclair resident founded the American Iris Sociey?

A. Frank H. Presby.

Q. Where can one view an extraordinary collection of plants, trees, and shrubs mentioned in the Bible?

A. Bible Gardens of Israel in Woodbridge.

Q. Where is the Aviation Hall of Fame, containing historic aircraft equipment?

A. Teterboro.

Q. What Newark park is noted for its lovely cherry trees?

A. Branch Brook.

Q. What physicist who produced the first nuclear chain reaction lived in Leonia from 1939 to 1942?

A. Enrico Fermi.

Q. The rare fringed gentian can be viewed at the Wet Meadow in what garden?

A. Skylands Botanical Garden.

✦

Q. Which famed anthropologist spent her childhood at 338 Fairview Avenue in Hammonton?

A. Margaret Mead.

✦

Q. What nuclear physicist, "the man who built the atomic bomb," directed the Institute for Advanced Study at Princeton from 1947 to 1966?

A. J. Robert Oppenheimer.

✦

Q. What happened to New Jersey's blueberry crop on May 21, 1992?

A. Half of it was destroyed by a late freeze.

✦

Q. What famed aviator was married in Englewood on May 27, 1929?

A. Charles A. Lindbergh.

✦

Q. What is the state bird?

A. Eastern goldfinch.

✦

Q. The mountainous area in the northeastern part of the state is part of what large, multistate region?

A. The Appalachian Mountains.

Q. What kind of topography covers three-fifths of the state in the southeast?

A. Coastal plains.

Q. How many acres of forested land does New Jersey have?

A. 1,985,000.

Q. What is the state tree?

A. Red oak.

Q. What builder of the Brooklyn Bridge is interred at Riverview Cemetery in Trenton?

A. John A. Roebling.

Q. Who was "the Wizard of Menlo Park"?

A. Thomas Alva Edison.

Q. What Cumberland County town is "the dandelion capital of the world"?

A. Vineland.

Q. What coffee company, whose slogan is "Good to the Last Drop," has headquarters in Hoboken?

A. Maxwell House.

Q. What astronaut and recipient of NASA's Distinguished Service Award spent his childhood in Oradell?

A. Walter M. Schirra, Jr.

———◆———

Q. What pharmaceutical genius established a plant in Rahway in 1899?

A. George Merck.

———◆———

Q. Where can flower lovers enjoy more than 6,000 varieties of iris?

A. The Presby Iris Gardens in Mountainside Park, Montclair.

———◆———

Q. What are the high ridges in the Piedmont plateau called?

A. The Palisades.

———◆———

Q. What is the only endangered species of fish in New Jersey?

A. Short-nosed sturgeon.

———◆———

Q. What is the state flower?

A. Purple violet.

———◆———

Q. What are the tide-worn quartz pebbles found on the beaches at Cape May Point called?

A. Cape May diamonds.

Q. The Wings and Water Festival is held in which South Jersey town every September?

A. Stone Harbor.

———◆———

Q. Where is the purest water supply in New Jersey?

A. The Pine Barrens.

———◆———

Q. Where are the national offices of the Textile Research Institute?

A. Princeton.

———◆———

Q. What college, founded in Hoboken in 1870, specializes in science and engineering?

A. Stevens Institute of Technology.

———◆———

Q. Alfred Stieglitz, the "Father of Modern Photography," was born in what New Jersey town in 1864?

A. Hoboken.

———◆———

Q. What unusual bird arrived at Stone Harbor in 1958 and has stayed there to nest and flourish?

A. Glossy ibis.

———◆———

Q. What inventor, who laid out the town of Hoboken in 1784, developed the world's first seagoing steamboat, the *Phoenix,* which operated to Philadelphia in 1809?

A. John Cox Stephens.

Q. Where was the first steel pen factory established in the country in 1858?

A. Camden.

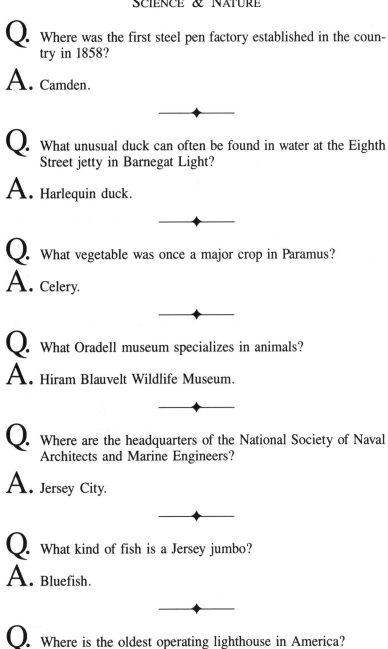

Q. What unusual duck can often be found in water at the Eighth Street jetty in Barnegat Light?

A. Harlequin duck.

Q. What vegetable was once a major crop in Paramus?

A. Celery.

Q. What Oradell museum specializes in animals?

A. Hiram Blauvelt Wildlife Museum.

Q. Where are the headquarters of the National Society of Naval Architects and Marine Engineers?

A. Jersey City.

Q. What kind of fish is a Jersey jumbo?

A. Bluefish.

Q. Where is the oldest operating lighthouse in America?

A. Sandy Hook, which began operation in 1764.

Q. Where is the Plastics Institute of America situated?

A. Hoboken.

———◆———

Q. What park hosts a Crab Apple Festival each May?

A. Ringwood State Park.

———◆———

Q. What forerunner of the U.S. Coast Guard had its headquarters at Sandy Hook?

A. U.S. Life Saving Service.

———◆———

Q. Where in 1899 did Guglielmo Marconi give his first demonstration of the wireless telegraph?

A. Navesink Light Station.

———◆———

Q. What Metuchen physician made major contributions to public health?

A. Ezra Hunt.

———◆———

Q. Where is the Wetlands Institute?

A. Stone Harbor.

———◆———

Q. What Newark pharmacist developed a popular talcum powder?

A. Gerhard Mennen.

Q. What Whitesbog resident pioneered the cultivation and marketing of blueberries and cranberries?

A. Elizabeth White.

Q. What Rutgers University graduate and microbiologist wrote *My Life with the Microbes?*

A. Selman Waksman.

Q. What New Jersey entomologist discovered the Japanese beetle?

A. Harry B. Weiss.

Q. Vladimir Zworykin, inventor of the iconoscope, died in Princeton in what year?

A. 1982.

Q. The third American to orbit the Earth was what Hackensack native?

A. Walter M. Schirra, Jr.

Q. What eminent ornithologist and curator at the American Museum of Natural History was born in Englewood in 1864?

A. Frank M. Chapman.

Q. The famous gorge in the Kittatinny Mountains has what name?

A. Delaware Water Gap.

Q. The first scientific paper on communication with extraterrestials was published in 1959 by what Somerville man?

A. Philip Morrison.

———◆———

Q. What scientist, born in Woodbine in 1903, was co-discoverer of the birth control pill?

A. Gregory Pincus.

———◆———

Q. What county has the oldest county park system in the United States?

A. Essex.

———◆———

Q. What wildlife sanctuary is famed for its rare orchids?

A. Bennett Bog Wildlife Sanctuary in Cape May County.

———◆———

Q. When was the New Jersey Audubon Society incorporated?

A. 1910.

———◆———

Q. What is the largest salamander in the state?

A. Tiger salamander.

———◆———

Q. One of America's first soap manufacturers was what Jersey City man?

A. William Colgate.

Q. What city was once known for its production of locomotives?

A. Paterson.

———◆———

Q. Lobbying by what Cranford activist secured passage of the Pure Food and Drug Act in 1906?

A. Alice Lakey.

———◆———

Q. Small geese called brunt spend their winters in what New Jersey location?

A. Barnegat Bay.

———◆———

Q. What unit of the Forsythe Wildlife Refuge is noted for attracting winter raptors?

A. Brigantine.

———◆———

Q. Where was John Walter Christie, inventor of the first amphibian tank, born in 1865?

A. River Edge.

———◆———

Q. Peter DeJongh, designer of the Oak Ridge installation, died in what New Jersey town in 1983?

A. Kearny.

———◆———

Q. What rare snakes are often found in the Pine Barrens?

A. Scarlet and pine snakes.

Q. In what county do most of the few remaining bears in the state live?

A. Sussex.

Q. What two types of New Jersey turtles live on the land?

A. Box turtle and wood turtle.

Q. Pan American Airways founder Juan Terry Trippe was born in what small New Jersey town in 1899?

A. Sea Bright.

Q. What New Jersey city was once America's preeminent manufacturer of silk?

A. Paterson.

Q. For using a catheter to chart the heart's interior, what Orange-born physician won a Nobel Prize in 1956?

A. Dickinson W. Richards, Jr.

Q. Montclair was the birthplace in 1930 of which astronaut, the second man to walk on the moon?

A. Edwin ("Buzz") Aldrin.

Q. What noted herpetologist and author of the book *Snakes I Have Known* was born in Newark in 1876?

A. Raymond Ditmars.

Q. What fort on Sandy Hook was used by the U.S. Army as a proving ground from 1874 to 1919?

A. Fort Hancock.

———◆———

Q. Where does New Jersey rank as a cranberry-producing state?

A. Third, behind Massachusetts and Wisconsin.

———◆———

Q. What shore bird, a variety of snipe, is easily recognized by its enormous eyes?

A. Woodcock.

———◆———

Q. The hull of what ship is a state historic site?

A. The *Atlantus* in Cape May Point.

———◆———

Q. What Newark-born man founded Lockheed Aircraft?

A. John Northrop.

———◆———

Q. What coins did New Jersey mint in the 1780s?

A. "Horse Head" coins.

———◆———

Q. Where is the Thomas H. Kean New Jersey State Aquarium situated?

A. Camden.

Q. Where are the New Jersey Audubon Society's headquarters?

A. Franklin Lakes.

———◆———

Q. What popular show is held every spring in the National Guard Armory in Morristown?

A. New Jersey Flower and Garden Show.

———◆———

Q. Where does New Jersey rank in the number of hazardous waste sites?

A. First, with 109 sites.

———◆———

Q. What South Orange man is credited with establishing the standard time zones for the United States?

A. William F. Allen.

———◆———

Q. Where was telephone service first provided in the state on August 15, 1878?

A. Camden.

———◆———

Q. Caspar Wistar built America's first successful glass factory in what New Jersey county in 1717?

A. Salem.

———◆———

Q. What natural insulator, once abundant in Barnegat Bay, is making a comeback?

A. Eel grass.

Q. What controversial sex researcher was born in Hoboken in 1894?

A. Alfred Kinsey.

———◆———

Q. A pioneer in the use of preventative inoculation, what physician vaccinated the people of Trenton for smallpox in the 1740s?

A. Dr. Thomas Cadwalader.

———◆———

Q. What state park, west of Matawan, includes 450 acres of salt marsh?

A. Cheesequake.

———◆———

Q. The first city in the world to be lit by incandescent bulbs was what Union County community?

A. Roselle.

———◆———

Q. What Sussex County borough was the site of the nation's first anthracite furnace in 1841?

A. Stanhope.

———◆———

Q. What barrier island is found four miles off the coast of Ocean County?

A. Long Beach Island.

———◆———

Q. What environmental organization owns nearly one thousand acres of wetlands in Avalon?

A. World Wildlife Fund.

Q. In which Union County town was three-in-one oil developed?

A. Rahway.

———◆———

Q. Where can the piping plover and other endangered birds be seen nesting during the summer?

A. The Holgate Section of the Forsythe Wildlife Refuge.

———◆———

Q. What area, covering nearly 25 percent of the state's land area, is the last remaining wilderness between New Hampshire and Virginia?

A. The Pine Barrens.

———◆———

Q. What peninsula is referred to as an island because it is surrounded by water during high tides?

A. Cattus Island.

———◆———

Q. Which New Jersey waste site is considered the worst in the country by the Environmental Protection Agency?

A. Lipari Landfill in Pitman.

———◆———

Q. In 1929, what Middlesex County town became the first community in the United States to have a cloverleaf highway intersection?

A. Woodbridge.

———◆———

Q. What is the highest temperature ever recorded in the state?

A. 110 degrees on July 10, 1936, in Runyan.

Q. What is New Jersey's only native cactus?

A. Prickly pear.

———◆———

Q. What is the name of the six-mile-long sand spit north of Highlands?

A. Sandy Hook.

———◆———

Q. How many Fortune 500 companies have their headquarters in New Jersey?

A. Twenty-three.

———◆———

Q. What bayoulike garden of water plants can be enjoyed in Saddle River?

A. Waterford Gardens.

———◆———

Q. What diesel-air submarine can be seen at a berth in Hackensack?

A. USS *Ling*.

———◆———

Q. Where is the Museum of Glass?

A. Wheaton Village in Millville.

———◆———

Q. What Ocean County town is the western terminus for the world's first fiber-optic transatlantic cable?

A. Tuckerton.

Q. What shore town has an internationally known bird sanctuary?

A. Stone Harbor.

———◆———

Q. Hoboken was the birthplace in 1895 of what Depression-era photographer, known for her documentary pictures of the unemployed?

A. Dorothea Lange.

———◆———

Q. What unusual plant was discovered in the Pine Barrens and grows almost nowhere else?

A. Curly-grass fern.

———◆———

Q. When was the first ferry service opened between Hoboken and Manhattan?

A. 1811.

———◆———

Q. What is New Jersey's official state animal?

A. Horse.

———◆———

Q. What nature preserve has views of Silver Bay and Barnegat Bay?

A. Cattus Island County Park.

———◆———

Q. What Paterson schoolteacher built the first submarine, the *Holland,* in 1898?

A. John Philip Holland.

Q. What Paramus museum contains specimens of various indigenous rock formations?

A. Bergen Museum of Art and Science.

———◆———

Q. Who demonstrated America's first working steam locomotive on his Hoboken estate in 1824?

A. John Cox Stevens.

———◆———

Q. What is the seventeen-trillion-gallon lake under the Pine Barrens called?

A. Cohansey Aquifer.

———◆———

Q. Where are more than 6,000 acres of freshwater wetlands under federal protection?

A. Great Swamp near Chatham and Summit.

———◆———

Q. What is the name of the black basalt cliffs that tower above the Hudson River?

A. Palisades.

———◆———

Q. In what marshy basin have more than 270 species of birds been observed?

A. Hackensack Meadows.

———◆———

Q. What is the state insect?

A. Honeybee.

Q. Where are some of the finest flatwater canoe streams in the northeast found?

A. The Pine Barrens.

———◆———

Q. For what topography is the Brigantine National Wildlife Refuge noted?

A. Salt marshes and barrier beaches.

———◆———

Q. What did the iron furnaces at Batsto produce to help the army during the Revolution?

A. Munitions.

———◆———

Q. Where does the endangered peregrine falcon nest?

A. Forsythe National Wildlife Refuge.

———◆———

Q. What museum in Oceanville houses a fine collection of decoys?

A. Noyes Museum.

———◆———

Q. What yellow-orange flower found in Hacklebarney State Park is shaped like a tiny lantern?

A. Jewelweed.

———◆———

Q. What is the coldest temperature ever recorded in the state?

A. Minus 34 degrees on January 5, 1904, in River Vale.

Q. What gardens contain climbing hydrangea, golden oriental spruce, and a dwarf iris?

A. Skylands Botanical Gardens.

———◆———

Q. What now-restored former ironworks town is a tourist site in central New Jersey?

A. Allaire Village.

———◆———

Q. What southern shore location is a notable nesting ground for egrets and herons?

A. Stone Harbor Bird Sanctuary.

———◆———

Q. Where is the Frelinghuysen Arboretum?

A. Morristown.

———◆———

Q. What fruit grower wrote the first American book on pomology in 1817?

A. William Coxe.

———◆———

Q. Francis Bacon Crocker, founder of the first school of electrical engineering in the United States, died in East Orange in what year?

A. 1921.

———◆———

Q. A favorite haunt of the snowy owl is what park?

A. Island Beach State Park.

Q. What Dutch-born engineer and pilot who designed aircraft for Germany in World War I died in Alpine in 1939?

A. Anthony Fokker.

✦

Q. In lower Delaware Bay what mammals calve each June?

A. Bottle-nosed dolphins.

✦

Q. What rare tree frog is found almost exclusively in the Pine Barrens?

A. *Hyla andersoni.*

✦

Q. Where does New Jersey rank among the states in suicide rate?

A. Forty-ninth.

✦

Q. Two million peach trees covered what county until an infestation of San Jose scale in the 1890s destroyed them?

A. Hunterdon County.

✦

Q. What wildlife management area is in Vernon and Hardyston townships in Sussex County?

A. Hamburg Mountain.

✦

Q. While working at the Bell Laboratory in Holmdel in 1929, what scientist discovered that Earth is bombarded by static from the Milky Way?

A. Karl Jansky.

Q. In the Pine Barrens, what is a fingerboard?

A. A place where several roads come together.

———◆———

Q. Despite its name, what type of land formation is Barnegat Peninsula?

A. An island.

———◆———

Q. What presently undeveloped state park is situated in Forked River?

A. Double Trouble.

———◆———

Q. What museum can be found in Allaire State Park?

A. New Jersey Museum of Transportation.

———◆———

Q. Where was America's first road sheet asphalt pavement laid in 1870?

A. Newark.

———◆———

Q. A fire tower tops what high point in the Pine Barrens?

A. Apple Pie Hill.

———◆———

Q. What natural site south of Cape May Canal has been called a "truly unique area of multiple habitats"?

A. Higbee Beach Wildlife Management Area.

Q. Among the states, where does New Jersey rank in the median age of its residents?

A. Fourth.

Q. What Burlington County site features freshwater tidal marshes and large stands of wild rice?

A. Rancocas State Park and Nature Center.

Q. Each April before vegetation emerges, where can one see the rubb, a shore bird?

A. Pedricktown Marsh.

Q. In what Salem County location can one see the beautiful American lotus (*Nelumbo pentapetala*)?

A. Mannington Meadows.

Q. What Morris County site is noted for wood ducks, barred owls, and bog turtles?

A. Great Swamp National Wildlife Refuge.

Q. Who wrote *New Jersey Coastwalks?*

A. D. W. Bennett.

Q. Where are the American Littoral Society's headquarters?

A. Sandy Hook.

Q. What South Jersey site has spectacular concentrations of Monarch butterflies during their autumnal migration?

A. Cape May Point State Park.

———◆———

Q. What New Jersey broadcast station was the first in the nation to televise a human image on August 13, 1928?

A. WRNY in Coytesville.

———◆———

Q. Where does New Jersey rank in number of state and local police per population?

A. First, with 39.1 police per 10,000 population.

———◆———

Q. Who invented celluloid, the first widely used plastics material, in Newark in 1870?

A. John Wesley Hyatt.

———◆———

Q. A birding area for cliff swallows and Acadian flycatchers is in which portion of the Delaware and Raritan Canal State Park?

A. Bull's Island.

———◆———

Q. What firearm was developed in Paterson in 1836?

A. Colt revolver.

———◆———

Q. Where can one find such unusual vegetation as red cedar, beach plum, and wild black cherry trees?

A. Island Beach State Park.

Albert and Shirley Menendez are residents of Gaithersburg, Maryland. Albert is the author of a number of books including *Christmas in the White House* and *Maryland Trivia*. A former librarian in Westchester County, New York, Shirley is now director of housing at Georgetown University.